Ghosts of Colorado

DENNIS BAKER

Schiffer
Publishing Ltd

4880 Lower Valley Road, Atglen, PA 19310

Cover photo by Andy Davies, 365images.com
Copyright © 2008 by Dennis Baker
Library of Congress Control Number: 2008927059

Designed by Stephanie Daugherty
Type set in Burton's Nightmare 2000/Copperplate32bc/NewBskvll BT

ISBN: 978-0-7643-3052-0
Printed in the United States of America

Schiffer Books are available at special discounts for bulk purchases for sales
promotions or premiums. Special editions, including personalized covers, corporate
imprints, and excerpts can be created in large quantities for special needs. For more
information contact the publisher:

Published by Schiffer Publishing Ltd.
4880 Lower Valley Road
Atglen, PA 19310
Phone: (610) 593-1777; Fax: (610) 593-2002
E-mail: Info@schifferbooks.com

For the largest selection of fine reference books on this and related subjects, please
visit our web site at
www.schifferbooks.com
We are always looking for people to write books on new and related subjects. If you
have an idea for a book please contact us at the above address.

This book may be purchased from the publisher.
Include $5.00 for shipping.
Please try your bookstore first.
You may write for a free catalog.

In Europe, Schiffer books are distributed by
Bushwood Books
6 Marksbury Ave.
Kew Gardens
Surrey TW9 4JF England
Phone: 44 (0) 20 8392 8585; Fax: 44 (0) 20 8392 9876
E-mail: info@bushwoodbooks.co.uk
Website: www.bushwoodbooks.co.uk

Dedication

This book is dedicated to my Mother, who created a rich environment for me as a child that helped foster my creative genes. And she, too, has had her share of ghostly encounters in her life.

Acknowledgements

Thanks to all who supplied photos: Andy Davies (365images.com), Brenda Bryne, Sheila Anderson, Michelle Baker, Kelly Goode, Marla Ginsburg, Sheron Bellio, Brian Leffler, Erin Steckman, Bryon Bonner, Clarissa Vazquez, Sarah Pierce, and most of all, Grandma and Grandpa Skultety.

Contents

INTRODUCTION: Ghostly Glory 7

HAUNT #1: What is a Ghost? 9

HAUNT #2: The Specters of the Stanley and the Baldpate Inn, Estes Park 23

HAUNT #3: Welcome to Hotel Colorado 36

HAUNT #4: Haunted Miramount Castle and Manitou Springs 49

HAUNT #5: Creepy Colorado Springs 52

HAUNT #6: Castle Rock, Elevated Fears 60

HAUNT #7: Morrison's Mysteries 64

HAUNT #8: The Devils of Denver 67

HAUNT #9: Black Hawk's Haunted Houses 82

HAUNT #10: Ghosts of the Silver Towns 85

HAUNT #11: Paranormal Platteville 87

HAUNT #12: Central City's Lady in Black 88

HAUNT #13: The Ghosts Aren't Fair In Fairplay 89

HAUNT #14: The Ghost of Georgetown 90

HAUNT #15: Ghostly Golden 91

HAUNT #16: Colorado's Alien Encounters 93

HAUNT #17: Grand Junction's Ghostly Encounters 99

HAUNT #18: Breckenridge, More Haunted Heights 103

HAUNT #19: Boulder's Haunted High and Other Spooks 105

HAUNT #20: Bigfoot Tales From The High Country 111

HAUNT #21: Creepy Canon City 119

HAUNT #22: Freaky Fort Carson and Fort Collins 120

HAUNT #23: The Apparitions of Arvada 123

HAUNT #24: Wicked Wheat Ridge.. 127

HAUNT #25: Haunted Highlands Ranch 129

HAUNT #26: Littleton, a Tale With a Bite! 134

HAUNT #27: The Northern Ghost of Longmont 136

HAUNT #28: Satan Calling? 137

HAUNT #29: Deep Fears On Barr Lake 139

HAUNT #30: Haunted Hamilton 140

HAUNT #31: Terror of Thornton.. 141

HAUNT #32: The Gorgeous Ghost 143

HAUNT #33: Frightening Florissant 144

HAUNT #34: Spooky Summit Springs 145

HAUNT #35: Ghost Gold of Poncha Pass 146

HAUNT #36: Alarming Alma 147

HAUNT #37: Wicked Wedding Bell's of Ouray.. 148

HAUNT #38: Eerie Elizabeth.. 149

HAUNT #39: Killer Kiowa 150

HAUNT #40: Floating Lady of Francisco 151

HAUNT #41: Monsters of Meade and Mesa Verde 152

HAUNT #42: Guardian Ghost of Saint Elmo 153

HAUNT #43: The Tools of the Trade 155

CONCLUSION: Colorado Haunted Tour Wrap-Up 158

Bibliography and Web Resources.. 159

Ghostly Glory

J agged cliffs hung with menace over the narrow road that twisted through mountainous terrain leading to Estes Park. Pine trees gripped solid rock as if holding on for dear life. I squeezed the steering wheel as the road twisted, leaving one clueless as to where they were or what could be around the next corner. This was not the first time I would be in sheer terror on that trip.

Arriving at the Stanley Hotel, I popped out of the car, breathed a sigh of relief, and headed to the lobby to check in. I paused for a moment, partly because the altitude left me searching for fresh oxygen and partly to take in the beauty of the landscape.

White cap mountains line the skyline touching billowing clouds as a sea of green pine trees cover the ground as far as the eye can see. One would not immediately associate this land with ghosts or hauntings. Nor should they, unless they, like I, turn and go into the Stanley—which is what I was about to do. The Stanley is only one of many haunted locations in this land of ghostly glory.

The top of the Stanley Hotel. *Courtesy of Andy Davies—365images.com*

In these pages, I will take you on a tour of Colorado's most haunted places and dive into some of its deepest mysteries. Use this as your tour guide if you are in Colorado. And if you stay at the Stanley, let's hope it's not room 403. Why? You will have to read on to find out.

Good luck!

HAUNT #1

What is a Ghost?

Hibbing Auditorium apparition.
Courtesy of ghost hunter Brian Leffler from the Northern Minnesota Paranormal Investigators

As a child, I never considered the scientific or philosophical aspect of the paranormal. I only knew what I had personally experienced. And that was truly something at the least, other worldly, at the most, an extreme venture into the power of the imagination. Let's consider the former for our purposes and explore the question, "Just what is a ghost?"

If we then propose ghosts are "something" and there is an over abundance of evidence supporting that, at the least, it is a noteworthy subject to pursue, just what *are* they? A riff in time where energy from the past or even the future crosses our own space-time continuum? The spirits of the dead wandering the earthly plane in pursuit of their former physical lives? Demons pretending to be ghosts for whatever reason? Let's look at each of the theories.

Ghostly form of human? The form of a man sitting in an auditorium.
Some spooks look like they did in real life.
Courtesy of ghost hunter Brian Leffler from the Northern Minnesota Paranormal Investigators

First, I believe that science, given its demand for empirical evidence, be taken into consideration. Science will only consider what it can "prove," which seems odd because they can't prove most of what they say they have evidence for. But nonetheless, from a scientific position, what can be said of a ghost?

Time, to me, is an intriguing consideration for the paranormal. What if ghosts are the energy signatures of the dead etched in the fabric of time itself? Some hauntings are "repeats," where a ghost is seen doing the same thing over and over again. This is called "Residual Haunting or Recordings." Is it possible that it is some yet unknown force in nature that is recycling an event in a process of physics we can't even comprehend?

Consider this perplexing theory. Scientists believe that space is filled with virtual particles; these particles, for no known reason (at least mathematically), come into and exit existence for reasons we can not explain and only to repeat the process again and again. This theory helps physicists feel more comfortable with the idea of the universe coming from "nothing." Personally, I believe in God, but there is nothing to say that God didn't create such mechanisms to create matter from empty space. Thus, based on the aforementioned, how could this be applicable to the paranormal?

The scenario I mentioned earlier, where many ghost stories are about predictable ghosts repeating a task, is similar to virtual particles. That is, no one can explain why either could happen, but both could have a scientific reason for why they are called *real*. Both are extremely far fetched and neither can be proven. So one scientific view could be some oddity of a natural repeating process in physics.

Here, consider what happens when you sit in the same spot for a good deal of time and then get up. What you leave is heat from your body and an impression in the couch you were sitting upon. Could the dead leave a signature behind? Is the soul an energy or essence left over from the living? This is assuming that ghosts have some material substance. It is possible that they are something completely otherworldly?

Ghosts could be the souls of the departed having nothing to do with anything in the physical world whatsoever. In this theory, consideration to Biblical perspectives are inseparable and very detailed in dogma when talking of the dichotomy of the body, soul, spirit, etc. We will not venture into those discussions, but in this

**This is believed to be
a ghost in the form of
a misty energy.**
*Courtesy of ghost hunter
Brian Leffler from the
Northern Minnesota
Paranormal Investigators*

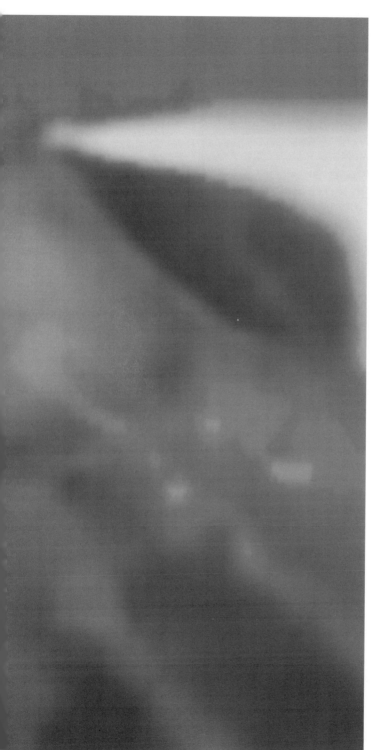

Scene from True Story of the Woodland Haunting documentary. Shelia Baker was attacked by what she described as a demonic force—a creature with burning red eyes. *Courtesy Mindsplinters Films, LLC*

theory, the bottom line is that the soul is "spiritual" and has nothing to do with the material world. Why you could see something from the spirit world, obviously is something no one can explain.

However, here the belief is the body dies, the soul lives forever, and sometimes the soul (or ghost) is left to wander the remains of their former life until moving on. But why would some ghosts stay behind?

Some think that perhaps a tragic event is the cause for a spirit to stay behind. Or perhaps the yearning for a loved one; maybe a bride-to-be who died on her wedding night. The theory is that some great emotion drives the dead to try and continue their earthly journey, yet now absent the body and any ability to fulfill their desires. Thus they are trapped forever on a vain quest never able to move on. But what if ghosts are something even more menacing than the spirits of the dead?

Many believe ghosts are demons trying to meddle in earthly affairs. In fact, the major religions forbid speaking to the dead for the simple fact that you have no idea who you are speaking to. An example is found in 1 Samuel in the *Bible*. King Saul used a medium to call up Samuel from the dead—something the passages describe as punishable by death. From a Biblical perspective, the scriptures layout that the world of the dead should never be used for practical earthly endeavours. If ghosts are the dead, what form do they take on earth?

The first most familiar is that of a human form, albeit transparent. That is you can, like in the movies, see through them. These ghosts resemble their former selves and seem to walk as if in contact with solid structures. Mostly, these sightings are quick visits and the apparitions disappear almost as fast as they came. Sometimes the human-formed ghost appears like you and me—that is, solid.

Stories of hitchhikers picking up strangers who disappear shortly after getting into the car have been floating around for years, some with a degree of credibility. These ghosts seem to have the ability to take human form completely. The solid ghost stories are the rarest of all.

The most popular type of sighting these days, however, would be orbs.

Orbs are those balls of light that appear on pictures or video footage. Most speculate that these are just light reflections in the camera lens, or maybe dust bunnies floating about—which they most probably are. However, there are a few orbs which defy explanation— like ones that move with some sign of intelligence in video clips.

Most ghost researchers seem to think that orbs are just "energies" of the deceased as mentioned before. These energies are possibly left over from the essence of the living.

Another type of ghosts are shadow people. These hold a more menacing presence than orbs or human-like ghosts. They are more associated with unpleasant hauntings where mischief abounds. I had the joy (if you can call it that) of seeing one of these as a child.

I had been out playing and came in the house for a break. As I stepped into the house, a large shadow figure, almost as tall as the ceiling, stood just feet from me. We locked eyes and I was unable to move for a few minutes. Finally, I gathered enough courage to make it out the front door. Returning later, it was gone. My encounter is typical of shadow-people sightings.

Mostly they appear in human form but are void of features. They are, essentially, a shadow. Some have reported a shapeless or swirling mass of blackness that appears and seems to be absorbed into the walls. And a few have said that shadow people have caused

There is a face on the left hand side of the tree. It was taken at Elmwood Cemetery in Brighton Colorado. *Courtesy of Erin Steckman*

Masonic Cemetery in Blackhawk, Colorado. This is the gravesite of the infamous "Cameron." Legend says that every April 5th and November 5th, his soul mate, a woman dressed in white, has been seen laying flowers over his grave. *Courtesy of Erin Steckman*

Shadow person streaking across the room. *Courtesy of Delaware Ghost Tours*

Castle Gate Apartments in Arvada, Colorado. This was interesting due to the detail it creates, like a claw or a hand. *Courtesy of Erin Steckman*

some disturbances like moving or breaking objects, but nothing like that of a poltergeist.

Poltergeist are the most feared of all ghost encounters. In addition to moving objects and breaking them, they have been know to cause harm to people, like scratching and even biting. In one famous case from the movie, *The Entity,* a poltergeist relentlessly harassed a young woman, and by some reports, raped her. These types of ghosts are fortunately rare.

Ghost then can be any number or perhaps all of these things. One thing is for sure, there is enough evidence to warrant that, at the least, specters and spooks just might be wandering around our worldly domain. This book deals specifically with one location on Earth—Colorado. I will tell you what I found out and what I personally experienced. I will begin with the Stanley Hotel in Estes Park, Colorado.

The Specters of the Stanley and the Baldpate Inn, Estes Park

In front of the Stanley. *Courtesy of Andy Davies—365images.com*

THE STANLEY HOTEL

My first location, which is by far not the least on my haunted tour, is the Stanley Hotel in Estes Park. I arrived at the hotel which presented itself as nothing more than an upper-class historic setting. In fact, it seemed quite cozy. And after a long drive, I was eager to sink into a bed and worry about finding out about ghosts later. It turned out I would not have to find the ghosts—they would find me.

Now before diving into the spiritual side of the Stanley, let's look at the history of this majestic structure. F. O. Stanley, inventor of the Stanley Steamer automobile, moved to Estes Park in 1903 on

orders from his doctor, due to battling tuberculosis. The move to the elevation improved his health significantly, so much so he felt a debt of gratitude and decided to open a hotel and thus help the local economy.

In 1909, the Stanley Hotel opened, an elegant, classy establishment of Georgian architectural style popular at the times.

The hotel was built on land purchased from English Earl Lord Dunraven. Dunraven came to Estes in 1872 in hopes of opening a hunting preserve. The Lord apparently swindled many locals out of money and land. But to the people of Estes good fortune, Stanley would not repeat such acts and, in fact, built the hotel on the very spot Dunraven planned a lodge.

After the hotel opened, many a famous guest ventured through its glamorous doors—President Theodore Roosevelt, The Unsinkable Molly Brown, John Philip Sousa, the Emperor and Empress of Japan, and many movie stars. In fact, the location would soon be a Hollywood favorite as a filming location.

Dumb and Dumber, Jim Carey's comedy, was filmed at the Stanley along with other films. Most people mistakenly think the "original" *Shining* was filmed there. It was not. Stanley Kubrik used various locations in the United States for the 1980 film, but shot most of the footage in the United Kingdom. However, the Stanley did have a role to play in the story.

Stephen King stayed at the Stanley while writing the original book which inspired the movie. King apparently hid away for five months in room "217," where he fashioned the

Outside the Stanley at night.
Courtesy Bryan Bonner,
Rocky Mountain Paranormal

story which even included the very room he was staying in. The hotel apparently fed a good deal of King's inspiration for the book—an inspiration the producers of the film did not share, and hence the film was shot elsewhere. King was apparently annoyed by this fact, but the 1997 miniseries did come back to the source of the story and was filmed at the Stanley. Of course, we are talking about a writer who created a fictional haunted story about made-up events. Is there anything really supernatural going on in the halls of this lavish establishment? The answer is: Plenty.

Flora and Stanley

Aside from my own experience, ghostly reports by hotel workers and guests of the hotel abound. Let's take a look at some of the best haunted stories about the Stanley.

Most notable of the disembodied residents of the hotel is F. O. Stanley himself. Mr. Stanley is said to have been seen in the billiard room and in the kitchen. Stanley seems to favor these locations for whatever reason. He is not shy either about appearing to an entire tour group in the billiard room and he frequently visits the bar, giving the bartenders a good look before slipping back into the netherworld. But F. O. of course wouldn't haunt the hotel alone—his wife, Flora, gives a hand.

Flora prefers the ballroom where it is reported she continues her piano playing; a big part of her life was spent entertaining guests of the hotel in that very room. Flora apparently enjoys performing for the new patrons as well.

Lord Dunraven, mentioned earlier, is another spirit with an affinity for a special spot.

Lord Duraven

Dunraven it is said likes to hang in room 407. He seems to like to be close to the bathroom for no particular reason and has a thing with flipping light switches on and off. If you keep on eye on the window from the outside of the hotel, you might even get a glimpse of Dunraven; it seems he likes to see what is going on in the exterior world and spends some time peering outside.

And so it appears the ghosts of the hotel have favorite spots to hang out. I have mentioned some of the more famous ghosts but there are rooms in the hotel haunted by "anonymous" spirits.

Room 401, a hot spot of ghost activity. *Courtesy Bran Bonner, Rocky Mountain Paranormal*

Room 418

Room 418 is reported to be where the youthful spirits like to consort. That is the room where cleaning crews have heard an abundance of strange noises and seen impressions on the bed as if someone were sitting on it. Guests of the room hear children play in the halls at night, and some have even checked out, being scared out of their wits. One ghost boy has been seen by tour guides, and even Stephen King himself reported seeing a disembodied boy in that very area. So if you stay in 418, remember that just might not be a soft spot in the mattress, it could be an other-worldly bed partner.

But room 418 is not where the list ends for frightful sleepovers.

Rooms 401 and 217 are also responsible for making guests edgy to the point of leaving the hotel. On the other hand, many visitors request these very rooms in hopes of sharing space with someone from the beyond.

A Night Inside The Stanley

These stories I just mentioned are all second hand; I wasn't there, so how can I know what really happened? You know what I mean: Aunt Elle sees a cat run past her one dark night and she thinks she sees a ghost. She tells Uncle Bill who adds that it had big red eyes. Bill tells his friend David who adds that it growled like the Devil himself and so on. How could "I" know the Stanley was haunted? I would have to spend the night—which is what I did.

I already mentioned in the Introduction something of my trip, but left out much of the detail. Let me shape the night I stayed in words that can hopefully set the mood for you, should you decide, when I am done, that you still want to make reservations.

Crisp fall winds made leaves dance across my driveway as I pulled my 150,000-plus miles Jeep onto the road. She was well driven but solid. The trip started uneventfully—a long stretch of Colorado's treeless highway, a quick stop to grab a cup of coffee, and a final glance back to the endless plains before making my way through the mountain passes.

The road to Estes Park where the Stanley is located twists and turns in a dizzying fashion. The other factor I had to deal with was the additional distraction of the awesome beauty of the landscape; it is tempting to stare off and admire the handsome cliffs, the sparkling rivers that follow the drive, and the occasional wildlife that curiously watches travelers. But common sense held my hands tight to the steering wheel all the way to the Stanley.

On first glance, I was not that impressed with a frightening terrain. Although I had seen the pictures of the Hotel, I envisioned something more menacing, something more like in the original movie, *The Shining*. Driving up, it was cold but sunny, the hotel elegant, clean, and anything but scary looking. Entering the lobby, however, would give me a different impression.

The first thing I noticed was that the interior of the hotel was mostly wood. The design gives you a feeling of another time—as if you stepped into the past. Or maybe it is the past coming to you. But there was a definite feeling of something odd I couldn't nail down. I passed the feeling off to the history and the stories, especially those from the movies and Stephen King's book. It was a little like walking into the pages of his story. The feelings promptly faded as I went through the business of checking in.

There is something about pulling out your Visa that dampens inspiration and spiritual matters. But monetary exchange is the necessary evil no matter where you are. Quickly enough, however, I had things wrapped up and a bell boy was carrying my bags to my room.

The bell boy dropped my bags at the front door, I tipped him, and soon made my way inside the room. Tired from the drive, I was eager to sleep. I peeled the sheets back and dove in. Nothing this fresh smelling or comfortable could be haunted, I thought. The hours would soon prove me wrong.

A Welcoming

It was just after midnight; I remember because of the glow from the alarm clock bothered me, but not enough for me to turn over and unplug it. I did, though, notice the time when I first felt a gentle shake of the bed. I thought nothing of it at first. If you have ever been in California when a quick earthquake rolls almost unnoticed, that was what it was like. One odd shake I can understand, but it keep repeating.

About every fifteen minutes, the bed felt like someone was trying to wake me up by jerking the post. It was working because I was becoming more and more alert and aware that something was up. I sat up and reached over to retrieve my glasses on the night stand. Before I was even near them, I heard something airborne—it was the very glasses I was reaching for.

My eye glasses had taken flight and landed on the other side of the room. I jumped up and stumbled around in the dark until I found the light switch. The lights came on—and stayed on—I found my glasses, and from what I remember, may have left those on as well. The rest of the night went event free.

That is my Stanley experience. Some bed shakes and flying eye glasses. If I was trying to find evidence of a haunted hotel in Estes Park, I certainly found what I was looking for. The Hotel offered much more than chilling moments, as I discovered the next day.

The Shining Revisited

I snaked my way through the halls of the Hotel, soaking in the environment like dry sponge when it meets a puddle. Each area I ventured into brought a flush of scenes from *The Shining* to mind.

I made my way down the staircase leading to the lobby. As I did, I kept imagining a ball bouncing past me as it did in the series. And perhaps I would turn and be face to face with a child apparition. That did not happen. But the same flash-back type feelings continued as I ventured into the bar area.

I leaned over the bar which was empty since it was morning and looked at myself in the mirror. I almost felt like the bartender and Jack Nicholson were right there, and I was listening to Jack getting advice on a choice of drinks and how to murder his family. I knew this was not the same hotel as in the movie, and that the TV series was filmed here instead, but the imagery from the book, the movie, and TV all seemed to blend into my imagination for the most wonderful

Stairs as seen on the ABC TV mini-series, *The Shining,* filmed at the Stanley.
Courtesy of Andy Davies—365images.com

Lobby at the Stanley. *Courtesy of Andy Davies—365images.com*

macabre experience. I left Jack and the bartender to their discussion and sunk into the basement.

When I was there, I missed the ghost tour; of course, I had already met one of the ghosts, so I wasn't disappointed. The basement displayed an interesting wall with information about various movies shot at the location. It did not feel particularly scary; but it was nostalgic in many ways.

THE BALDPATE INN

The Stanley was not the only haunted joint in town. The Baldpate Inn also offered something more than friendly service.

The Baldpate Inn had more humble beginnings than the Stanley. Gordon and Ethel Mace built a cabin for themselves and several other cabins for income. The move proved profitable and they decided to open an Inn. The Inn officially opened in 1917, and one of the more interesting things about this haunted spot is in its name.

The name Baldpate comes from a fictional inn in which guests had their own private key to the building. And the Maces not only named their Inn after the one in the story, but gave their guests their own keys just like in the novel. They did this until WWI when metal was rationed for the war effort. When they stopped giving out the keys, guest began bringing keys to the Inn—lots of keys—in fact, to the tune of some 20,000 or more now. A room was dedicated to the collection, hence the name, "Key Room."

But the real story of the Baldpate is similar to the Stanley; the founders are still there.

The Maces still hang out in the Inn according to reports. Ethel it seems didn't like booze while she was alive and still doesn't. Be careful of your drink at the bar because it might just spill on its own. And, at the price of cigarettes, it is not recommended you bring any with you as they could come up missing. Mr. Mace had a disdain for smokes and he will quickly dispatch yours if you bring them along.

A Side Trip to The Elkhorn Lodge

The Elkhorn Lodge close by is also said to have a spooky guest, and one worker says he has the picture to prove it. At least he *did* have the picture...

The Elkhorn was built in 1874, a couple years before the Custer massacre. A worker who recently was in the building taking pictures had a strange experience. He took an Instamatic shot for his boss of a teepee. The shot popped out of the camera. He watched it develop and supposedly got more than he bargained for.

No one was in front of the teepee. Yet in the photo, a very tall man appeared, dressed in western garb holding a whip, albeit a little transparent. The worker quickly tried to get the attention of someone else to verify what he was seeing. However, by the time he was able to share his curious photo, the ghostly figure had all but faded. He told a co-worker what the man looked like, and oddly enough, the description matched a one-time local stagecoach driver who was very tall.

To Sum It Up

My experience there? The only thing odd was that my jeep window was "shattered" early in the morning. It was strange; no debris to indicate something smashed it, nothing, just shattered. Was it due to some other worldly force taking its anger out on my vehicle, or just natural, yet unexplained, causes? The only thing for sure is I will never know about that or anything else I experienced in Estes Park!

Did my glasses really fly across the room on their own? Was something shaking the bed? Or was it all something I imagined, attributed to exhaustion, something I ate, or watching to many episodes of *Ghost Hunters*.

I lean toward believing it was *something*, but you will have to stay there and decide for yourself based on your own experience.

I checked out of the Stanley all too soon. Though not there long, I was happy to have had some supernatural experience. Pulling out of the parking lot, I could see the hotel in my rear view mirror. It truly looked like a post card. I sped off in search of breakfast and more haunted locations in Colorado.

Next stop, Glenwood Springs.

Welcome to Hotel Colorado

Hotel Colorado, Glenwood Springs, Colorado. *Courtesy of Clarissa Vazquez*

T he Stanley gets the press because of its association with *The Shining* and continuous visits from *Ghost Hunters*. But it is not by any means less haunted than my personal favorite ghostly hotel, the Hotel Colorado—not only because of the paranormal happenings in the structure itself, but because of the history of Glenwood Springs and the unique ways to get there.

My sisters and I took a train "up" the mountains to reach Glenwood. The trip was simply fabulous with a special car designed just for viewing the scenery. The train twisted and hung on narrow ridges all the way to the famous city of Glenwood where Doc Holliday's bones rest somewhere in a graveyard a short walk from the train station. *Ole Doc,* in fact, died in Glenwood in the Hotel Colorado, probably one of the most haunted places in the west.

Nestled at the base of tall, rugged mountains, Glenwood is a beautiful city. It is everything you would expect from a tourist stop for curious travelers. It is also known for something much more than just a spooky hotel—its water.

Glenwood is host to natural hot springs which bring in guests from the world over to bathe in the buoyant waters for its supposed medicinal value. I personally floated for an hour and just felt salty and wet. But I would guess it is the perception of the individual which leads you to believe you have had a benefit from the waters or not. Similarly, it is the individual who must decide if this town is host to visitors from the after life. I will first give you some history, then tell you what happened to me.

A Historic Town

The history of the land has the makings for a great movie and sad real-life story. The Ute Indians were the first to settle Glenwood. The name *Ute* came for the healing properties of the mineral waters; waters they called "Yampah" which means "Big Medicine." The Ute hidden paradise was soon invaded by the white man.

The United States Government assigned an agent, Nathan Meeker, to help modernize the indigenous population. Meeker failed to help the locals with his farmer advice, but did manage to grow their anger so much that they killed him and his comrades in

Former morgue in the basement. *Courtesy of Clarissa Vazquez*

what is known as the "Meeker Massacre." This event eventually lead to the government sending troops to route out the Utes, sending them to reservations in Utah.

The Indians, however, did not take to being driven from their land lightly. Since they could not fight back physically, they decided to make a stand in the spiritual world. It is said they placed a curse on the land. The details are sketchy at best. But, ever since that time, strange things have happened in many locations in the area. However, the focal point of most eerie tales surrounds the Hotel Colorado.

The town was originally called "Defiance," but the name was changed by Isaac Cooper to Glenwood Springs after he purchased a large plot of land. Cooper sold the property where Hotel Colorado now stands to Walter Devereux, who with his brothers, made a great deal of investments in the new town, building ornate pools and hotels on land scarred with a turbulent past.

But the stories I shared above are just a few of the reasons why ghosts could roam this land. The hotel itself has many a tale all on its own.

Hotel Colorado opened in 1893. It was designed to be a luxurious experience. Only the finest was used in the Hotel Colorado; expensive furniture, décor, and electricity, which was, at the time, rare for any building. Even the staff had a touch of class about them. The hotel did not hire locals as they considered them on the crude side. Instead, they reached out to as far as London to bring in professional staff, and it is no wonder, considering some of the hotel's guests.

Presidents Roosevelt and Taft, along with other famous folks such as Al Capone, stopped by for a visit. But for our interests, we are not concerned with the living that graced this majestic establishment, but rather the dead. And from the tales and my own personal experience, the dead are "alive" in the joint.

Hotel Colorado. *Courtesy of Frontier Historical Society*

Walter and Lucas

Walter, mentioned before, is believed to haunt the halls of the Hotel. But Walter left the Hotel and spent his final years in Maine and California. Another former owner's spirit could stalk the guests—that is the ghost of a Mr. Lucas.

Lucas took control of the Hotel Colorado in 1893, and became the owner in 1916. He later died in 1927, all of his later years filled with keeping watch over his hotel. Could it be Mr. Lucas still has interest that the hotel is run the way he liked?

Before I share my story, I will tell you some of the famous, and not so famous, tales about this haunted hot spot. Like the Stanley, the dead seem to prefer certain rooms. One such room at the Hotel Colorado is room 661.

Room 661

Room 661 seems to have a woman wearing a floral dress who likes to stand over guests as they awaken. It is not clear if different guests who stay in the room see the apparition and report it unaware

A rather large "orb" can be seen in front of the mirror. The doorway to the left is the entrance to the attic. To the right is room 515. *Courtesy of Clarissa Vazquez*

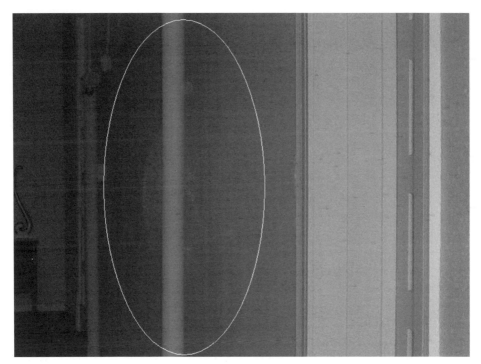

A possible apparition in the area of room 515. High EMF readings were gathered in this area at the time of this photo. The circled area is for easier viewing of the phenomenon.
Courtesy of Clarissa Vazquez

of similar events. Is it possible foreknowledge of the ghostly woman could cause people to imagine what they have heard about? Of course, but it is also possible she really does visit room 661 and simply enjoys watching folks sleep. When I heard of this story, it eerily reminded me of something that happened to me.

My Own Side-Story

My story has nothing to do with the hotel or even Colorado. I was in Tennessee at my Mom's house when I was awakened by a strange ghostly woman. I had spent the night during a visit in the early 90s. I stayed in a room by myself and woke to the smell of coffee and a woman whispering in my ear, "Den, the coffee is done." The voice spoke gently. I turned and walked out within seconds of the voice. Entering the dining room my stepfather greeted me, "Coffee is ready."

"Yeah Mom just told me," I said matter of fact like.

"No she hasn't said anything; she is in the shower…"

So I know what it's like to have a ghostly visitor to your bedside. But at Hotel Colorado, the ghosts are simply more, "a peeling."

Room 551

It is reported that when the Hotel tried to wallpaper room 551, the unseen occupant didn't like it, as the freshly-applied paper was in a pile on the floor the following morning. This happened more than once, in fact.

The room is also rumored to have a faucet that turns on by itself, lights that have a mind of their own, knocks at the door when no one is around, and even the TV likes to come on when it feels like it. So for a good time, stay in room 551; just don't choose this room if you are trying to get some sleep, is *my* advice.

Even Disney has been touched by the ghost of Hotel Colorado. In 1993, while filming in the area, one of the Disney workers went to the front desk to thank them for unpacking all of his items and even hanging suits in the closet for him. The folks at the front desk were perplexed and explained that the hotel never touches personal items of the guests. It appears the Disney crew had some unseen assistance, perhaps otherworldly fans of Mickey Mouse?

More Rooms to Haunt!

Room 324 is another great place to spot ghosts, even if not in their entirety. In the 90s, a guest reported opening the door to the room and seeing just the torso of a male ghost. It apparently stood there (even in the absence of legs) for several minutes until vanishing. Does this story have a leg to stand on?

Rooms 558 and 555 have yet more reports—TVs that change channels on their own—and while I don't know what channel they ended up on, I can only guess it was something scary like *Ghost Hunters* or a Paris Hilton reality show. But it is apparent that the unseen guests of the hotel simply like to play with worldly goods.

I mentioned that a Disney worker reported all his clothes neatly hung in the closet, something no earth-bound flesh was responsible for. It seems there is also a neat-freak ghost prowling the premises. Another person reported that disheveled books had stacked themselves when she walked into the another room. I don't know, but I wonder if they were alphabetized. Being a clean freak is not the only vice of the ghosts of the hotel, however.

It seems that some of the ghosts still want to hang on to earthly pleasures. One guest reported an apparition toting a cigar. The guest said you could even smell the cigar smoke. It's one of the things that distinguishes this haunted location from others. The dead have this

Hallway where we smelled the strange perfume. *Courtesy of Clarissa Vazquez*

On the train to Hotel Colorado.

seeming desire to play with objects from their former lives. Speaking of smells, I had my own encounter in the hotel halls with a smell whose origins were not of this world.

My sisters and I took a fall trip to Hotel Colorado a few years ago. We experienced some of what others had reported—one of which were the smells. Too excited to sleep, we roamed the halls late into the night, probably much to the dismay of other guests trying to sleep. Much of the time was spent joking around, but our jubilant behavior calmed on an unsettling event.

We strolled down one of the large halls, empty and dead quiet as we were the only ones awake. Grouped closely together, all of us stopped, curious of a strange smell. It was perfume, of course, but nothing the likes any of us had ever smelled before. It had more of a natural lilac scent. The smell drifted around the hall and then disappeared completely. There is a strange story surrounding the smell.

Lilacs and Florence

The fragrance is said to be from a woman murdered in the hotel. Her name was Florence. It seems Florence fell for a young miner from Aspen, as did another young woman. The other woman became jealous and put an end to Florence's life with a poker. The smell they say is what she wore (possibly) when she died. I don't know if it is her, but I do know the fragrance danced through the air as if it had a mind of its own. Perhaps it did.

We learned later that others had encountered the same smell. And thus the ghosts of this hotel continue to penetrate this earthly plain. Clean freaks, cigar smokers, wearers of pungent perfumes—what else could these meddlers of the material world be up to in the Hotel Colorado?

Haunted Elevator

The night we visited, our encounters included much more than smells. Near the elevator shaft on the second floor, you could feel something was wrong. A kind of sixth sense took over, as if we were feeling vibrations of the scene of a horrible accident. My sister, Sheila, said she saw a strange light emanating, as if there was a specter within the elevator chamber. I did not see it. But I did see the elevator move from floor to floor on its own.

My witness of the self-willed elevator is nothing new. For years, the staff has reported that the aged system moves randomly between floors, stopping and then moving on, as if someone was taking a ride. The hotel reports that most of the movement happens between 2-4 am. Perhaps even the dead prefer not to use the stairs.

Elevators are not the only choice of meddling of the spirits. They like to play with doors as well.

Doors are hard to keep locked at the hotel. In fact, they are hard to keep shut. The staff has reported the laundry room, locked up at night, will be unlocked and the door open in the morning. The same is true for the basement. In the early 1980s, a worker claimed that each

By the haunted elevator, Sheila and Brenda feel something strange.

The stairway, a twisting eerie trip.

night he would lock and shut the lights off in the basement. Upon returning in the morning, he found the lights on and the doors open. The basement is a haven for haunted tales at Hotel Colorado.

A Creepy Basement

During late night tours, guests have reported hearing a typewriter and women chatting in part of the basement. An investigation found no one was around. Other odd sounds have emanated from the basement that are mechanical in nature.

A security guard reported hearing the exercise equipment in use about two in the morning during one tour. At the same time, a guest he was escorting felt an extreme cold spot. His flashlight revealed no one was using the gym. I can tell you that the basement is one spooky place.

I ventured down there about midnight during my stay. The halls are long and dark, befitting almost any good horror film. As you walk the length of the basement, you hear squeaks and rattles that only drive your imagination. I didn't stay long; it felt foreboding to me and I was quick to leave. Of course, the lobby has no less an active history of the paranormal.

An Active Lobby

A public relations firm, during a photo shoot, snapped a picture of an apparition supposedly. The specter was sitting in a chair in the main lobby, dressed appropriately for someone in the late 1800s. The lobby also had some strange lights flashing about.

Once, staff reported that "flashes" of light, almost like that from a camera, flickered on and off in the lobby. No explanation or evidence was found as to what the lights could have been. Perhaps ghosts are mocking the living, reenacting the endless snap shots taken of the place in hopes of seeing a ghost. Plenty of orbs and other odd pictures have been taken, but of course, some are obviously fake, while others beg for explanation.

Other really bizarre events with lights have to do with candles.

Ghosts by Candlelight

The ghosts not only like to play with the modern lights, but they seem to fancy the lights of yesteryear. Candles have been reported sitting all over, a fresh flame tops each finding. And the staff has reported oil lamps burning well beyond the time they should have

run out of oil. No need to be afraid of things that go bump in the night; these spooks like to haunt in the light.

Doc's Death

Why would one hotel be haunted and another not? Perhaps it is in the history. Some I have already detailed. But more pain is in the years surrounding Hotel Colorado. It was used as a hospital in World War II—which of course included a morgue. Many a young man died in that place. Could the basement where the dead once lay be host to spirits? Perhaps they are the ones unlocking the doors and turning the lights back on? It could also be one of the famous former guest who passed away in the hotel causing mischief. That guest was none other than "Doc Holliday," the famous gunslinger who happened to also be a dentist.

Doc died in one of the guest rooms of "TB," a common fatal illness of the day. The hardened gunfighter avoided being shot at, hung, and other potentially violent deaths, to meet his fate slowly wasting away in a bed at the hotel. It was not the end he had expected; he believed he would die quickly. Perhaps his spirit lingers around the hotel, never satisfied with his unfortunate fate. If not the hotel, maybe he frequents the graveyard he "might" be buried in.

No one knows for sure where the good Doc is buried. I did walk the lengthy trail leading to what most certainly looks to be a haunted graveyard, where he might be buried in an unmarked grave. Even if he is not there, the graveyard is worth the hike.

The pioneer cemetery is filled with old head stones and has the look straight out of a Stephen King book. Even in the day time, it was a spooky place. I did not see anything, but my guess is that if you hung around long enough, you could run into a ghost—or they would run into you. But the haunting of Glenwood Springs doesn't end at the graveyard or the hotel.

Several other buildings in the city have a haunted reputation. Take a weekend and your camera to Glenwood Springs. And don't be surprised if you come back with a photo of a spook. I hear that you shouldn't be surprised if the spook even comes back with you!

After spending an equal amount of time tracking ghosts and floating in the hot spring waters, it was time to move on. We climbed on board the train and headed back to Denver.

Next stop, another town famous for spring waters and spooky locations, the famous Manitou Springs.

Haunted Miramount Castle and Manitou Springs

The trip from Denver to Manitou is a curious one. After driving through wide open plains, rustic mountains towering off to your west, you head straight for Pikes Peak, which is a menacing bald mountain sitting alone at the end of the Rockies. To reach Pikes Peak and Manitou, you can pass through the Garden of the Gods.

Garden of the Gods just might be haunted as well as some of its surrounding towns. Countless joy climbers have met the grim reaper while scaling the red skins of the peculiar stones that reach straight up to the sky, like hands trying to escape hell's fire, still red from the flames of the abyss. From the comfort of your car at the Garden, you can see in the distance a small town. You wouldn't have a guess as to whether ghosts live there; they do.

I am talking about the ghost of Miramount Castle in Manitou Springs. The city rests in the shadow of Pikes Peak, one of Colorado's most recognized mountain tops. The entire city is built on sharp inclines, including the Miramount Castle. This building is perched on the side of a hill and is one of the more unusual places I visited. Manitou is an odd location all on its own, but the Castle makes it even more strange. I like the location perhaps because Manitou was my first Colorado home.

Like Glenwood Springs, Manitou's first inhabitants were Indians. The name Manitou means "great spirit." The Indians considered the place sacred grounds and that sentiment lives on today. The town is a haven for spiritualist and new-agers seeking sanctuary. They too consider the town to have some type of energy or other-worldly significance. But when I made the town my home, I had no clue of any of this.

I was much younger, just into my twenties. I caught a bus and left Michigan, hoping for a better life in Colorado. I ended up living in a cheap apartment within walking distance of the Miramount Castle. My life in those days was consumed with just surviving; the supernatural is the least of your concerns when the natural is your focus—as in just eating. As a result, I never visited the location until more recently. It is an awesome piece of architecture.

The Castle came to be as a result of a French-born priest who came to Manitou in hopes of the mineral waters improving his

health in the 1890s. He had the Castle built from memories of his childhood travels with his diplomat father. I strolled through the building with keen interest as it was a unique piece of work. The only thing I encountered was some great treats at the gift shop. Not so with others who have visited.

Ghostly Inhabitants?

The ghost of a little girl has been seen walking through the halls carrying a doll. She appeared to come from another time, as she was dressed in attire from the early 1900s. Other ghosts from that time period seem to hang about as well. A Victorian-dressed woman and a stately-dressed man have been seen around the Castle. The ghosts could just be lost, as the Castle is a maze of staircases, rooms with strange angles, and a secret corridor the public is not allowed to venture into. The Castle does have at least one tragic death that could explain why a ghost would hang around.

The story goes, a nun had become pregnant. For whatever reason, she committed suicide—perhaps because of the ridicule of those around her. It could be her ghost playing with the lights and doors, as it is rumored they have a will of their own, like the Stanley. So is this place really haunted?

The Castle doesn't have as many reported sightings and strange phenomena like some of the other places in Colorado, but it is eerie to tour, and you just might get a peek of a specter if you are lucky—or unlucky as it were.

Racing Death...Hounds Aplenty

But the haunted fun of Manitou moves well beyond the Castle.

The town has its own "coffin race" the Saturday before Halloween each year called the Emma Crawford Coffin Race. Last year, over 5,000 folks made and hauled coffins up the hillside. Why? Emma died of TB in the 1800s. She was buried on a hill above the town, but years later rains washed her casket back to town. And this, of course, sparked someone to create a festival reenacting the event.

You can also get a "Hounds of Hell" tour as the town has many locations that are reported to be haunted. And there are other locations like The Cliff House, that while it doesn't have a reputation for being haunted, the building is old and the Victorian feel gives you a sense you've stepped back in time.

The Stage Coach Country Inn

Manitou has another spooky joint worthy of mention here that has a mysterious past—The Stage Coach Country Inn. Mysterious as in no one knows for sure what that past *is*. What they *do* know is that the location was a famous Inn as far back as anyone could remember. And they do know the adjunct house was built in 1881. But the details of a credible history are fuzzy at best, almost as cloudy as the ghost stories about the place.

Some people have said that the bed and breakfast has spirits that like to throw things at you. What and at whom no one seems to know. But other rumors say that the ghosts suck the warm air out of rooms, stomp around while you are trying to sleep, and are even violent.

Guests have reported being bruised by the abusive spirits of The Stage Coach Inn. But once again, who are these people? All too befitting a place with a mysterious past to have a mysterious present. So if you are one who likes to journey into the unknown, this could be your kind of place. If nothing else, they have a great reputation for fine food and dinning with a long list of famous folks who swear the eats are good there, and there is no mystery about that.

If you have ever been to Manitou, you will realize this is the last stand of the hippie culture, and the haunted "Mushroom Monday" resonates with that spirit—and perhaps a spirit of another kind.

The ghost of an old man, oddly enough, appears to walk up from the floor, finally to stand in front of you, and then disappears. No one knows why he comes up through the floor, but some suspect the near by bath house may have something to do with it. Could this be the ghost of a former bather? One thing is for sure, the bath house area presents a feeling of a long lost past waiting to be discovered.

The bath house was a magnificent spectacle to travelers in the 1890s with its grand Queen-Ann décor. Presidents McKinley, Roosevelt, and Ulysses S. Grant, all ventured there. As you walk around the building, you almost feel like you will be greeted by some apparition from better times. Well, who is to say you will not?

I would go to Manitou even if it didn't have haunted locations. It is for sure one the best places in Colorado to step into the past. And just maybe, the past will come to you!

Manitou's neighbor, Colorado Springs, has its own haunted reputation.

Creepy Colorado Springs

Also under the shadow of Pikes Peak is Colorado Springs. It was founded in 1871 by General William Jackson Palmer, who also founded the Rio Grande Railroad. Several haunted spots cover the landscape of the rustic-red earth land. With the beauty of natural wonders like *Garden of the Gods,* it is hard to imagine anything scary.

PIONEER MUSEUM

But nonetheless this land of beauty holds some haunted tales like those surrounding the Pioneer Museum.

The Pioneer Museum holds the history of the local Pikes Peak region which may include something more than artifacts. The structure built in 1903 served as the El Paso Court House for years. The grand architecture has been the scene of some horrific incidents, which could be why it is haunted.

Garden of the Gods.

In the 1950s, an employee, upset over a paycheck, mowed down his boss, killing him. This did not help the disgruntled worker resolve his pay issues, but did help foster rumors that the building is haunted by the ghost of the slain manager.

EVERGREEN CEMETERY

Another spooky spot at over 6,000 feet is the Evergreen Cemetery. It's such a rich paranormal environment that each year the *Evergreen Cemetery Benevolent Society* holds the *Victorian Spiritual Walk Through*. Take a candlelight tour to the past and see how ghost hauntings started in Victorian times.

BLACK FOREST

Another spooky spot near the Springs is the Black Forest. There just might be more in these woods than ticks and deer. Maybe something from beyond the grave. The story is about a local resident, Steve Lee. Lee reported some strange goings on which have had even the local police baffled.

Lee first reported strange noises in and about the area of his house. He has heard noises like someone dragging chains on his roof, as well as something that sounds like someone running in the woods. But his disembodied guest does more than just make noise.

Lee has also smelled a foul odor in his truck and seen strange lights in his house at night. But the strangest of all has to be the lights which he and others have seen, including prominent local politicians. Even the show *Sightings* has come back a few times because of the bizarre happenings in the area, and yes they do have photos. (Visit www.scifi.com/sightings/.)

Pictures of the lights have been captured. Local authorities will not say this is a ghost, but they do believe something is going on. As for Lee, he thinks it is the government with some sort of experiment. Whatever it is, you might just run into it if you hike into the Forest.

ST. FRANCIS HOSPITAL

If you are feeling ill while on your trip to Colorado Springs, beware of staying at St. Francis Hospital; reports have it the place has more than just health care in store for residents. The ghosts of St. Francis are vocal and they like to play pranks on the workers.

Many a nurse has reported a disembodied voice coming up behind them, always with the same question, "What ya doing?" in an old sailor-like tone. The ghosts appropriately haunt the old tuberculosis ward which probably was the last place many of them spent their time during their lives. But the spooks don't stop to just chat—they also like to play with the workers.

At least one employee reported being locked in a closet by a poltergeist prankster. Perhaps it was an accident, but the worker was sure it was an other-worldly trick. Is the place haunted? Most places that have been the scene of suffering and death seem to carry stories of paranormal activities. If St. Francis is haunted for sure, I couldn't say, but I know I personally would prop the door if I ventured into a closet.

For a more residential haunting take a short trip to the Lee residence.

LEE RESIDENCE

The Lee Residence is not a great place to take pictures. Many report that, after developing them, some come back with a mysterious green glow. In addition, an amateur ghost hunter caught orbs moving in what appeared to be intelligent patterns on film. He also discovered that his compass went haywire in one part of the house. Could that be some portal into the afterlife?

ANTLERS ADAM'S MARK HOTEL

Antlers Adam's Mark Hotel has reports of mysterious goings-on, as well as in Colorado Springs. The structure has been destroyed twice in its history. It was built in the late 1800s, but was destroyed by a fire at the turn of the century and rebuilt.

The new structure was grand and eloquent, and stood for decades only to meet an end to modernization in the 1970s. It was then torn down again. The structure that now stands is called the Antlers Hilton. Even though the building has been replaced several times, the "spirit" or spirits of the place have seemed to stick around.

It is said to be haunted by the ghost of a young girl who committed suicide on prom night in the 70s. But not all the ghosts are thought to have come from the modern building. Some believe the spooks have stuck around from previous structures.

The ghost of a woman in a flowing gown is also said to be seen coming down the stairs. With over 121 years of history, it's bound to produce a spirit or two. The woman seems to have no connection to a story from the living similar to the ghost of the hotel's bar.

Judge Baldwin's Bar serves spirits alright—one is a handsome well dressed gentleman who likes to hang out at the bar after closing. But all the ghosts of the Antlers seem to keep to themselves, aside from an occasional manifestation.

Now if you like your ghosts served speedily, the Springs has its own take-out joint that is haunted.

ARBY'S

Arby's is best known for super roast beef sandwiches, not the supernatural. But in one Arby's in the Springs, there are reports of more on the menu than food. It is reported to serve up scares of a profound kind.

Openers, those folks who come in alone in the morning, have said a woman mysteriously walks through the locked store and exits the back door. And the closers are not spared spooky encounters either.

Some hear a man call their names, but the big trick the poltergeist play is after the chairs are put on top the tables at night, you come back in the morning to find them all on the floor.

There was a murder on the premises in recent times, but this doesn't seem to be connected to the haunting.

Colorado Springs ghosts don't only stop at fast food for freaky encounters, they have even moved to retail.

KMART

Kmart has more than blue light specials in Chapel Hills, they have a diverse list of ghostly reports. Spooks are said to knock over displays, create cold spots and even brush up against workers early in the morning. Some believe it is the ghost of a former manager who is still trying to run things.

The Kmart haunting is pretty tame; for more elevated fears head to Helen Hunt Falls.

HELEN HUNT FALLS

Helen Hunt Falls is reported to be a place where several people die each year. In Colorado, deaths from climbing, skiing, and recreation are pretty typical. However, this location has some spooky goings-on, perhaps related to people meeting their demise on the rocky surroundings.

Some of those folks who came to an untimely end were the passengers of a tour bus that was destroyed by an earthquake. The

Helen Hunt Falls sign with gun shots.

roads snake in and out of tunnels in the area. When a driver noticed rocks tumbling down the hillside, he thought it was a landslide and darted into a tunnel to avoid them. Sadly, the tunnel collapsed suffocating all inside.

The bus is still buried in the tunnel, albeit the bodies have been removed. It is in that tunnel, and others, that people report strange things happening. Folks around the area say mysterious handprints appear on your car, voices call out at you in tunnels when no one is around. But for a ghost who like to pose, try and find the Green Lady.

The location is named after Helen Hunt who is buried somewhere at the top, close to the camp grounds. A hiker is said to have been taking stills along the trail. After developing the pictures, one displayed the form of a woman with a greenish glow sitting in the weeds. Could this be Helen herself? Take a hike and you may have a chance to ask her for yourself.

A School for the Deaf and Blind

Colorado Springs also is home to a school for the deaf and the blind. Students have reported seeing things in the basement. Indeed those who can hear have heard the strange noises from the ghosts that show up in the basement, dorm, and gym.

But the students at the former Garfield Elementary have more to fear.

Garfield Elementary School

It was some forty or more years ago when two third graders decided to take their lives in the Elementary. The kids committed the act in one of the rooms downstairs, where you can still smell the dead bodies—supposedly. And some say the kids' ghosts are still there.

People have heard them talk, or felt a cold chill that could be them standing nearby. Others have even said the pranksters have pulled their hair. The school is no longer an Elementary, though for these two, school is still in session, perhaps until the end of time.

But if you think this story is all washed up, visit Coronado High School.

CORONADO HIGH SCHOOL

In the early 70s, a life guard talked his girlfriend into staying after hours for a late-night swim. She had her little sister with her but that didn't interfere with his plans of romance—he just had the little girl swim while they made out in the office. Things did not go as they planned.

The little girl drowned, unable to get the attention of the lovers who were more concerned with passion than being responsible. Now people say that, in the early morning, you can see the ghost of the victim sitting in the pool. And some swimmers have complained of "something" brushing against them in the water.

DAYS INN

For travelers who stay at the Days Inn, you will want to avoid room 207, because it is haunted. Of course, that means anyone reading this book will want to stay there. The curtains have been known to open on their own and a strange thumping sound can be heard coming from within the empty room. Even the staff don't like to clean it.

A GHOSTLY NIGHT CLUB

Maybe you will need a drink after staying at the Days Inn and hearing the ghost of room 207. But be careful, one of the night clubs is haunted in town as well. An unnamed club was the scene of a horrible death in the 1950s. The owner hanged himself in the basement. Employees say he still "hangs" about, showing himself or whispering to them.

LIBERTY HIGH SCHOOL

Liberty High School auditorium is another spooky place where learning and lingering spirits meet. The ghost of a worker killed during the construction is reported to turn the lights off and on, and if you are real quiet, you can hear him fall again from the catwalk where he met his end many years ago. And Liberty is not the end of the haunted school tales.

PALMER HIGH SCHOOL

Some thirty years ago, a student at Palmer High School hanged after getting cut from a role in *Macbeth*. Ever since, whenever the school does the play, strange things happen that sometimes doom the production. And in 1998, a noose was seen hanging above seats that had been rattling on their own. Still, the show must go on; that is, unless this story is true.

MONTGOMERY WARDS

The location of the old Montgomery Wards (now a hospital building) has a story, if only the walls could talk, and some say they do. Shoppers at the one-time retail outlet say that strange noises would come from the walls. But it got really weird when you went to the ladies room.

Women reported toilets would flush and faucets turn on by themselves. This was before the days of auto plumbing. But the strangest story that belongs in a legends and myth book is that of "the missing children."

The story goes that a mother and father let their kids go to the restroom alone in Wards. They waited, but the kids never came out. An investigation proved futile; the kids were never found. Is this story true? If you go into the restroom, they say you can still hear them…Perhaps they slipped into another dimension. Then again, this could be a tall tale made up by…children.

MORE GARDEN OF THE GODS

And back to Garden of the Gods; it was an old Indian burial ground. The spirits are apparently not too happy about that. Cars die for no reason, and blue orbs can be seen from time to time.

Not as big as Colorado Springs, but a few hundred feet higher and perhaps more haunted is one of my favorite places in Colorado, Castle Rock.

HAUNT #6
Castle Rock, Elevated Fears
THE WOODLAND HAUNTING 2

I am fond of Castle Rock partly because I lived there for seven years—but also because it comes with a good deal of history for haunting and it is where I filmed most of *The Woodland Haunting*. That is where I will start out, ghostly encounters while filming the movie.

The film was really low budget, most of the ghost and haunted special effects were filmed in front of a green screen. An odd thing occurred in the middle of the picture.

Each night after filming, the bright lights would be turned off on the set. We would turn them off for fear of fire because of the energy it takes to run them. Upon returning each morning, the lights would be back on again. This happened time and time again. I had heard of something similar on a Hollywood set as well. My guess is that ghosts have an affinity for film and it appears budget is not a deciding factor in what to haunt. In all the years I lived in Castle Rock, that was my only haunted experience. However, the town is full of tales of ghostly happenings.

CANTRIL SCHOOL

Cantril School, as it was formerly called, now the offices of the Douglas County School District, has a special guest. The school was built in 1896 to replace the original one that burned down and is reported to be host to a ghost who goes by the name, Matilda.

Matilda, it is said, lives by the furnace room—and walks the halls at night, her footsteps echoing when no one is around. No one knows why the ghost is named Matilda, but it really doesn't matter. If you visited and she made a loud thunder-like noise, like she did to an entire class room on one visit, the last thing you would want to know is her real name.

The old Cantril School is not alone in Castle Rock when it comes to spooky old places.

Mindsplinters Green Room, Actress Courtney Palm from the movie, *The Woodland Haunting 2*. This is the famous green screen room where lights had a mind of their own.

VICTORIA'S HOUSE

The Victoria's House is another haunted location in the heart of downtown Castle Rock. It is presently the Castle Rock Chamber of Commerce. Andrew Anderson purchased the property in 1896, where he and his wife raised their children, one of whom was Victoria. Sadly, Andrew and his wife didn't live there long.

Andrew died in 1901, and his wife passed a few years later. Victoria inherited the house and married, remaining in the location until her death in 1942. Her body rests in the Cedar Hill Cemetery today. (This location, by the way, was another set for *The Woodland Haunting 2*.) But while her body peacefully lays in the ground, her ghost just might still be at her old home.

Catherine Thornton, a Chamber employee, reported that late night calls would be picked up to "dead silence." And while the phones are quiet, the house itself certainly is not.

Employees have said they've heard what sounds like a hive of bees in the upstairs bathroom. Some hear snoring late at night with no one around. And it appears that Victoria is doing more than making noise as things have moved around on their own in the house.

According to Deb Tucker, events coordinator at the Chamber, a steel cabinet door opened unassisted while everyone watched. Could this be Victoria? On your visit to Castle Rock, stop by 420 Perry Street and find out for yourself.

Not only is the Chamber of Commerce haunted, but some of the city's local businesses report spooky events as well, like the Old Stone Church.

OLD STONE CHURCH

The Church was built in 1886, home to the St. Francis of Assisi Catholic Church. The site served as a church until 1966, when it was vacated for a new building. It remained empty until 1975, when it was remodeled to be a restaurant. And yes, they serve "spirits" there now.

It is reported to be haunted. One of the most often sighted specters is that of a little girl. While many patrons have seen the ghost girl, one boy in particular gave a detailed description which included, "something wrong with the back of her head." Could the girl have met some horrible fate on the grounds? No one knows. What they *do* know is that bizarre things happen there befitting scenes from Stephen Spielberg's *Poltergeist*.

Staff reports the lights doing strange things, objects that fly into mid air all on their own, chairs that move with no one around. Oh yes, spirits certainly *are* served in the Old Stone Church, whether you want them or not. Feel free to stop in for a bite.

CASTLE PINES GOLF COURSE

For those who like to have a good haunting and get their golf game in, Castle Rock even has its own spooky green at Castle Pines Golf Course. It appears that on fairway one, there is a cottage they tell of—a haunting that really stinks.

Staff has reported while cleaning the showers that a playful ghost turns on the water. Items are moved about frustrating anyone trying to tidy up the place. But most odd of all is a hideous smell akin to rotten eggs that really make this haunting so pungent.

SOUTH ELEMENTARY

A more gruesome haunting in Castle Rock is that of South Elementary.

The property behind the elementary has a bridge that holds a horrific tale. For some reason, men escorted small children over the bridge and into the woods where they all burned to death. Embellished or made up, if you are still and very quiet, you can stand on the bridge and hear the distant voices of men mixed with youth. Could this be cries from the past drifting through time? No one really knows, but you can go listen for yourself.

Castle Rock, I am sure, has more than what is chronicled here. In fact, it is a haven for UFO and Bigfoot sightings as well. A walk downtown, past the old buildings, you may hear the echo of voices from the past—voices slowly being silenced from new construction and the mass influx of tourists and new residents. The ghosts may just well leave Castle Rock some day because they won't recognize the city.

But one Colorado town has stayed the same for decades, the city of Morrison.

Morrison's Mysteries

We jump in our car, and after a short drive up a steep incline, we enter a small town that you could miss if it were any other place. But it has so much tourist activity, it begs for one to stop and see what is going on here. For its size, Morrison, on any given day, can be host to more tourists than one could think the city could hold. Morrison sits like a mouth entering the belly of the Rockies.

The town is about the same size in terms of sprawl as it was 150 years ago when it was founded by a Denver businessmen. However, the population swells with tourists on any given weekend—both the living and the dead.

HORTON HOUSE BED AND BREAKFAST

Horton House Bed and Breakfast is a charming, and sometimes alarming, place to spend the night. The front yard is crawling with structures looking more like a Tim Burton film than a lawn. The spookiest thing about the joint is the stories you will hear over morning coffee and pastries.

The most prevalent story is that of Amy who hung herself in the late nineteenth century in the carriage house behind the lodge. The reports are that Amy wanders the rooms of the lodge causing mischief and disrupting the peace of the living.

Amy is just the headliner of the phantom follies. The town is said to be teaming with spooks.

MORRISON HOLIDAY BAR,
RED ROCKS GRILL, AND MORRISON INN

One local called it an "infestation" of spirits. Morrison Holiday Bar, Red Rocks Grill, and Morrison Inn all report ghostly pranksters. The staff, such as bartenders, report regular events. For example, in one location, it's purported the ghost of a young dead girl targets barkeeps passing by with a small swinging gate. She apparently aims for the males' sensitive areas, which is I guess why they believe the spirit to be a girl.

The hauntings go well beyond the bars and inns.

LACEY GATE'S ANTIQUE SHOP

Lacey Gate's Antique Shop has a long-standing reputation for active poltergeist. In fact, the janitors refuse to go in after dark. The playful phantoms mess with everything from inventory to wiring.

CLIFF HOUSE

Another inn, called Cliff House, is said to be haunted by a young man who, like Amy, hung himself on the premises. Just a short walk from the Cliff House, you will find a very odd looking tree stump that, yes, it also said to be haunted.

The stump is in a lot, and like it sounds, it is just a stump. But, after dark, locals say the stump is a magnet for unwanted paranormal activity. Why? Well, the fact that it was the official "hanging tree" for the town could have something to do with it.

If all this isn't odd enough, this little town has two other ghosts with names and colorful histories.

THE HATCHET LADY OF RED ROCKS

AND COLOROW

The Hatchet Lady of Red Rocks is an eerie story your kids will love to hear before bedtime. It is said she lies in wait for an unsuspecting child and then drags them to her cave where she dismembers them and, of course, eats their flesh.

Her ghost has a close neighbor, Colorow, a Ute Indian chief who also haunts the high grounds over Morrison.

So what can be said of Morrison? Is this place really haunted?

This is probably the most haunted or most organized publicity effort of any of the Colorado towns. You may not *find* as many ghosts as you *hear* about in the town, but one thing you will find is a good time. To hear more of these tasty tales, go during Halloween on a Morrison Haunted History Tour.

For a city with plenty of room for ghosts to stretch out, we move down to the valley, where Denver has numerous haunted tales.

HAUNT #8

The Devils of Denver

We leave Morrison passing endless bikers heading for the town's taverns, twisting down steep grades and riding the brakes as much as the gas pedal. In the distance, still a good ways from Denver, sky scrapers reach up from the valley—the modern buildings a far cry from the city's beginnings.

Denver was born in the late 1850s after a mass influx of settlers in search of gold forced the federal government to organize some local order. Thus, the territory of Denver was born. The wealth dug up in Denver lead to the building of some elegant structures—some said to be haunted, like the Brown Palace.

THE BROWN PALACE

The hotel opened in 1892 by Henry Brown who, while on route to California, stopped in Denver. His wife liked Colorado so much, she told him to press on to California if he wished; she was staying in Denver. And so Henry stayed to amass a fortune.

He was one of the richest men in Colorado in the late 1800s, worth over five million dollars. His money didn't effect how he dressed, however. He liked to dress down in common cowboy attire. In fact, the way he dressed is what started the Brown Palace in the first place.

Brown walked into The Windsor Hotel in Denver dressed like someone who walked off the set of Ponderosa. The Hotel escorted him out and managed to enrage the wealthy tycoon. His revenge was to open his own hotel which is where The Brown Palace got its start.

Throughout the years, the Palace has enjoyed success and has been host to important guests, many of whom report the place serves up more than just lavish facilities. On the menu of things to be seen at The Palace is something best served *chilled*.

One ghostly tale is about a guest who lived in room 904 from 1940 to 1955. She apparently had significant suffering in her love life, possibly causing her troubled soul to hang around the room after she had died. The switchboard received calls from her empty room after her departure.

The story goes that a tour of the hotel included her room and her story of heartbreak and death. Oddly enough, once they stopped including her tale of tortured love the calls ceased.

Another sighting is that of a train conductor who likes to walk through walls. If you visit the airline ticket office, you might see him. The location was once where the train ticket office was housed. Apparently, the conductor is still offering rides, to where, no one knows.

If seeing a train conductor ghost isn't music to your spiritual ears, maybe this is. One employee walked into a room to find a band of ghostly musicians playing. The employee, stunned, asked them what they were doing, only to hear, "It's okay, we live here." And live there, they indeed do. And you can spend the night with them.

Each year the Hotel hosts the "Sleep With a Ghost" package. With the package, you will depart, satisfied with a grand tour, fine dining, a booklet of the hotel's ghost stories, and just maybe, you will depart with some ghost stories of your own.

If you didn't see any ghosts at The Palace, you can still stay in Denver and perhaps catch a spook at Molly Brown's old place.

THE UNSINKABLE MOLLY BROWN

Molly, as you may know from history class, was one of the few survivors of the Titanic disaster. While she did escape a watery grave, the reports are she still haunts her old elegant home in Denver.

The house is an eclectic stone home, an architectural mix of Classic Queen Anne, Romanesque, and refined neoclassical. It was built in 1889. Molly and her husband James Brown, purchased the 7,000 square foot, three-story mansion. How the Browns came into money is a story worth repeating.

The couple both came from poor, working-class backgrounds. James worked in mines, eventually working his way into a management position. Molly was a common store clerk. But their fortunes changed when James bought a mine of his own.

It just so happened that the mine he bought had a rich vein of "pure" gold. In fact, it was producing 135 tons of gold per day at one point and was called the biggest gold strike in history at the time. This changed the Browns—they were suddenly rich, which enabled them to buy their mansion. You might just call them lucky, that is until you consider their dream vacation.

It is hard to image the luck of picking a husband who happened on a mine that would make you filthy rich and picking the one vacation cruise that would be one of the biggest tragedies in history. That is exactly what happened. Molly had the best and worst of fortunes with choosing a trip on the Titanic.

But as Molly's luck or fate would have it, she was one of the survivors of the sinking. Her personal life inspired philanthropic activities and brought her recognition well past her death. And it seems maybe Molly is still getting attention these days from the afterlife.

The mansion is said to be haunted by the Browns. Staff has reported James is still smoking those God-awful cigars of his. No one is allowed to smoke on the premises—at least not the living. And Molly has been seen in her room, as well as many cold spots felt about the house, attributed to Molly's ghost hanging about. Molly is not the only ghost in the place, though.

Another female ghost is said to be in the dining room. Some have seen and even photographed the entity, although I couldn't find any pictures. She also is said to like to rearrange the chairs at the dining room table.

Another spook likes to play with the blinds, raising and lowering them. And if you're lucky, or unlucky, like Molly, you might just meet an angry spirit as you look into one particular mirror near the stairs on the first floor.

Molly died at the Barbizon Hotel in New York City. She is buried in the Holy Road Cemetery on Long Island. You can visit her grave or the Brown home where she still resides.

THE BELL WORDEN HOUSE

Bell Worden's House is another place where a ghost roams in Denver. The ghost of one John Fitzgerald is said to haunt the joint. And it appears John has a good reason to still be prowling about.

The house was once a whorehouse where Mr. Fitzgerald was paying for a service when he met his untimely demise in the spring of 1884. John slept in the bed of a prostitute when Madam Bell Worden and two other prostitutes stabbed him to death. After taking his money, they dumped him in the streets. The murderers paid for their crime as does everyone who visits the Worden House.

For those who like more of the old west in their haunted house head to the Bombay Club.

BOMBAY CLUB

The owners of the 1895 tavern called the Bombay Club say that the ghosts of cowboys still linger around the place. Both the living and the dead enjoy the "spirits" of the club.

If your taste is the more malevolent spooks, go to the Peabody Mansion.

PEABODY MANSION

Denver's Peabody Mansion is host to many spirits as well. The Mansion was built by former Colorado Governor James Peabody, but the haunting started many years after the good Governor was gone.

A young woman was reported to have been raped in the basement and another committed suicide in one of the bathrooms. These tragedies later lead to rumors that the mansion was possibly haunted by these two victims and with good reason.

A night club moved into the Mansion in the 1980s and the spirits were served in more ways than one. Many patrons reported strange things occurring in the place. And those who know the history of the mansion, believe the haunting is the result of the events of the past.

But if you want to raise your pulse a bit head to the Peccora House.

THE PECCORA HOUSE

I include this house in the book even though it no longer stands, as it was burnt to the ground for good reason. This was the scene of one of Colorado's most horrific crimes.

Guiseppe Peccora began the cruel tale by doing something that is hard to imagine. It was the 1870s; Peccora had the oddest means for a living. He abducted young boys, more than likely runaways, and made them work for him, playing music in the streets of Denver.

By trade, he was as a scissor grinder, but enslaving the young men provided supplemental income of sorts. It is not known how Peccora really treated the boys, albeit enslavement surely is bad enough. What is known is that on October 21, 1875, nothing could have matched the cruelty of what someone did to Peccora and his boys.

Someone broke in and slashed the throats of everyone in the Peccora house. Police found their bodies slumped, sitting in vast pools of blood. It is said that when a crime of this magnitude befalls a home or location, that the place is cursed. And that may be just what happened.

After the crime, the neighbors began to hear the odd chaotic harps of the boys mixed with desperate screams coming from the abandon home. And that was just the beginning. Those passing by could, on occasion, see dark forms roaming throughout the house. It was enough to drive some neighbors out and others to take more desperate action.

Finally fed up with the poltergeist of Peccora, someone decided to end the house of horror's misery. The place was burnt to the ground. If you wish, you can venture to Lawrence Street in Denver where it once stood, and on a late quite night, you may just hear a harp or a scream.

But if it's as quiet as a tomb, maybe Cheesman Park will give you a good scare.

CHEESMAN PARK

Denver's Cheesman Park, these days, you wouldn't want to visit alone; it's not the dead to worry about, but the living. It is not in a good area. In fact, it may have never been. The origins of the park was all about death.

The site was first called the Mount Prospect Graveyard which opened in 1858. Later they called the location Boot Hill, and then the city officially renamed the place City Cemetery in 1873. The residents of the graveyard are mostly criminals, transients, and victims of epidemics. Needless to say, they were not the beloved of the city. But what happened to their bodies, even the dead did not deserve.

The city wanted the bodies moved from the park to another large cemetery. What they did is hard to believe. Movers dug up the corpses

and placed them into one-by-three-foot pine boxes. Of course, you can not fit most bodies in that space, so they took to chopping up the bodies and cramming them into the small caskets.

It was reported to be a horrific scene that would make even Stephen King queasy, I am sure. Body parts were littered about the grounds, and some poor soul's arms were placed in boxes with another person's head. It was a scene sure to upset even the dead— and it was rumored it did.

Grave diggers reported freakish events. One worker said while removing a body, a ghost "jumped" on his back; he ran for dear life, lucky he lived to tell the tale. Near by neighbors reported ghosts wandering through their homes and soon the area was in an upheaval of chaos. Something had to be done.

In addition to problems with spirits, the city had trouble with logistics of the move, and finally, a decision was made to end the work. A mass grave was dug and the remaining bodies dumped and covered up. Trees and grass were planted over the burial site and eventually it was turned into a park. A park built on the bones of the dead.

After that tale you might not be surprised to run into an angry specter at the park while on your morning jog. I would be angry too if, after being dead, I was dug up, chopped to pieces, and then dumped into a hole, only to have the living play on the ground above. So if you venture to Cheesman and run into a ghost, give it a break; it was a hard life, and an even harder death.

Denver has plenty of horrific tales, some of more modern times.

CROKE-PATTERSON-CAMPBELL MANSION

Croke-Patterson-Campbell Mansion is home to one of the strangest and scariest haunting tales in all of Denver. The haunted tales date to the 1970s when new owners took over the building. At night, while no one was working, the sound of typing was heard echoing through the halls of the vacant building as it was being remodeled. The owners decided to use guard dogs to protect the property from intruders. It was a bad call—at least for the dogs.

The dogs couldn't even protect themselves, much less the premises. They found both dogs dead on the side walk, the result of

Croke Patterson Mansion, creepy exterior. *Courtesy Bryan Bonner, Rocky Mountain Paranormal*

a nasty fall through one of the buildings upper-level offices. Some believe something scared those pups to death. And the tragedy did not stop at the animal world.

A baby died in the nursery in the building, followed by the mother who committed suicide. The place was shortly thereafter turned into a museum, and you can, in fact, visit it now, if you dare. You see, you might be seeing more on your visit to one of Denver's scariest mansions than historic architecture; you may just run into whatever scared two Doberman Pinschers to death.

But if you wanted to see some of Denver's ghost in a more "timely" manner the spooks at the courthouse house are very punctual.

DENVER'S COURTHOUSE

It was 1900 in Denver's charming courthouse. A week-long event established this building in Colorado's haunted history. At exactly 3am every night for almost a week, the guards and janitors reported numerous ghosts walking and smelling up the second floor. The smell they said was sulfurous, which leads one to think perhaps these specters came straight from hell. Some of the hellish residents looked familiar.

Turret Room ceiling in the courthouse where ghosts were seen walking.

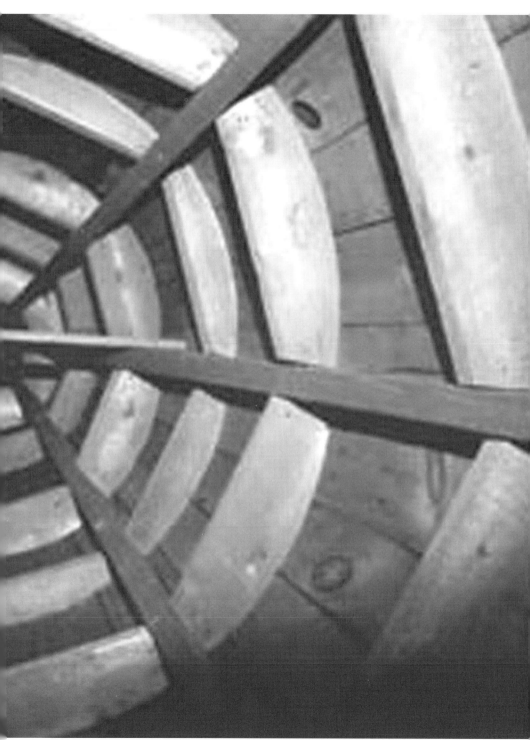

Courtesy Bryan Bonner, Rocky Mountain Paranormal

According to the workers, some of the dead were people who had been in the building while they were alive. One was said to be the elevator operator who met his demise falling into the shaft of the very elevator he worked in. Others, perhaps, were those sent to their deaths as the result of trials. Why did they come at 3am each night? No one knows. It did, however, lead to two of the workers quitting their jobs and moving out of Denver altogether.

So if you dare, slip into the courthouse, and *if* they let you, at 3 AM, sit by the doors on the second floor. You may just get a peek into the past, if Hell's court is adjourned and the dead released to wander the halls.

If you don't see anything, venture down the road a bit to Dunning Mansion, another active place.

DUNNING MANSION

Dunning Mansion is yet another of Denver's numerous hot spots for spooks. This haunted place is said to be infested with poltergeist. Folks have reported flying objects moving about on their own. And strange sounds from beyond drift through the air.

While there may not be a known reason why Dunning is haunted, Denver's International Airport has plenty of reasons why ghosts walk through its high tech architecture.

DENVER INTERNATIONAL AIRPORT

Denver's world class international airport sits alone in the vast plains outside the city. But the weary travelers who pass through the airport everyday may be in the company of the former residents of the land.

Native Americans lived here and considered the grounds to be sacred. And nothing could be busier than an airport to be plopped down in the middle of what you feel are holy grounds.

Are the native spirits upset? The local Indians held a ceremony to put their ancestors to rest. Don't be surprised, though, if you run into an Indian warrior spirit in line at Seattle's Best Coffee Shop.

For more travel-related spooks in the mile-high city, you can head down to the main train station in the heart of Denver.

UNION AND DENVER DEPOTS

Union Depot is a magnificent place. Movies like *Silver Streak* have been filmed there. I mentioned earlier in the book my train trip to Glenwood Springs; this is where that trip began. And I could not have thought of a more appropriate place to start a haunted investigation trip than Union Depot, because it, too, carries a significant history of haunting.

Ghosts have been seen wandering the vast chasm in the belly of the Depot. Some see the ghost of a solider, perhaps from one of the World Wars; others see a poor lost soul aimlessly wandering about the place, possibly reminiscent of a real life adventure through the station? Whatever spooks are present now, it is nothing compared to the ghosts that were said to haunt the original Denver Depot which no longer stands.

Denver Depot was torn down and replaced by Union Depot in 1880. It was said to be home to a pest of a poltergeist who, in life, was a three-fingercd hobo. The spook would tap relentlessly on the glass of the ticket counter. And at night, after 2am, you could see the ghastly ghost of the three-fingered hobo standing on the platform, and sometimes, he would walk through the offices unsettling the night workers. In fact, many quit, and some say the station was torn down over this one spook's determined effort to harass the living. Is the Union still home to this hobo? No one knows; you could always catch a train one late evening and find out for yourself.

GRANT-HUMPHREYS MANSION

We are not done with Denver yet, the place has more haunted locations then Paris Hilton has shoes. For example, the Grant-Humphreys Mansion has at least five or more ghosts hanging about the place.

Governor James Grant built the house in 1907, and sold it a few years later to the Humphreys. Today, the location is home to the Council on the Arts, but it is also the subject of ghost tales told, starting around Halloween. Why would this place be the subject of ghost stories?

On May 8, 1927, A.E. Humphreys, known as an excellent marksman, died from a gunshot wound. It was suspicious that

Grant-Humphreys Mansion. *Courtesy Bryan Bonner, Rocky Mountain Paranormal*

Inside the Mansion. *Courtesy Bryan Bonner, Rocky Mountain Paranormal*

someone so skilled in firearms would die from carelessness handling his own guns. The accident happened on the third floor, and if indeed he was murdered, his restless soul has reason enough to wander the spacious home. But his is not the only presence said to be in the home.

It is believed that up to five spooks have permanent residence in the home. In fact, local radio station KNUS sponsored a séance to talk to the ghost of Grant-Humphreys Mansion. Did they make contact? Who knows? Sometimes events are staged, but this place being haunted is probably real.

LITTLETON TOWN HALL OF ARTS

Another ghost-filled joint in Denver's suburbs is the Littleton Town Hall of Arts. If you work in this building, you have a great excuse for a messy desk. The ghosts here like to dishevel desks and mess up the place. But the real mischief begins when the work is long over and everyone has gone home—everyone but the ghosts that is.

Late at night, the haunted ghosts laugh and make music. The audible apparitions must think the place is still a theatre. If you hang

out late in the old ballroom, you might get front-row entertainment from the afterlife.

After your entertainment, head to the Buckhorn for a bite.

THE BUCKHORN EXCHANGE

The Buckhorn Exchange, now a restaurant, was once a trading post. But now there are more than just waiters attending to your table; it is said that the ghost of long-dead fur traders give guests grief by suddenly pushing the table while patrons eat a meal.

THE DENVER CHILDREN'S HOME

In the late 1800s, many orphans resulted from the hardships of life in those times. The Denver Children's Home was supposed to be a refuge for those homeless youth, but instead became a place of horror.

A fire broke out in the home taking the lives of several of the kids in the attic and upper floors. To this day, people tell of odd occurrences that happen, and some believe it is because of the tragic event.

Reports of seeing ghostly children and hearing their whimperings are numerous. But the most shocking apparition is that of a women in a long gown that floats down the fifty-foot-long hall. No one knows who she is, but after the fifth exorcism, the dead still hang around to haunt another day.

VETERANS OF FOREIGN WARS

The VFW has its share of ghost tales as well in Denver. They don't seem to bother you too much unless you want to watch music on TV. The current owner reported that late one night, while watching music TV after hours alone, the channel would change on its own. It happened several times, always moving to a non-music channel. It would seem the ghosts there don't like rock and roll.

In the basement, they report hearing loud rapping noises where many old war artifacts are kept. Some date all the way back to the Spanish-American War. The veteran specters also make an appearance now and then in the hallway.

MONK MONASTERY

If ghosts of former soldiers are not your cup of tea, you might want to step into the Monk Monastery for a religious experience. The apparition of a Monk is said to walk the roads around the Monastery.

Leaving Denver, we head back to the mountain range that lines the western sky as far as the eye can see. We head once again up the highway with signs warning truckers of the steep grades. But no warning of our next stop where seeing a ghost is something you can bet on.

Black Hawk's Haunted Houses

Many of Colorado's mountain towns have long lost their historic veneer. Instead, you will find ornate tourist traps basking in the lights of casinos. I found my way to one of these towns and quickly found more than I was looking for.

I actually went in search of cheap prime rib. And, in fact, I found a ridiculously low-priced dinner. I sat enjoying my meal atop a balcony dining area overlooking a sea of slot machines, all glistening from the lights bouncing off their chrome skins. A far cry from this town's humble beginnings.

John H. Gregory discovered gold in what was western Kansas territory; the area became known as "Gregory's Gulch." A number of small towns sprang up in the Mountains where it is located. One has a history of hauntings—Black Hawk, "City of Mills."

Today, the city is a well known for having a number of casinos. But among the massive new gambling establishments, you can bet you will find something a little more on the paranormal side. That would be The Lace House.

LACE HOUSE

The Lace House is just a few years shy of being as old as the town itself. It was built in 1863. Some of the locals say "everyplace" in Black Hawk is haunted. But the Lace House has the best reputation and stories to make it the focal point of the most-feared joint in the small mountain town.

Tales about the house abound, telling of creaky footsteps following you upstairs, and faded figures looking back at you in the mirrors. But the local police may have the best story of all.

Officer Al Ellio responded to an alarm that was triggered at the Lace House. He and his partner entered the house and turned off the alarm. They both stood in dead silence, feeling the kind of eerie calm you experience after a loud noise is suddenly stopped. As they stood, both heard a women and a child laughing upstairs in the house. They drew their guns and walked up the stairs.

Haunted Lace House. *Courtesy of Hauntedcolorado.net*

Creeping up the old stairs, they entered nothing but completely empty rooms. No one was there, but both men swear they heard the woman and child. The alarm has gone off several times since, he said, but no ghostly gestures followed.

Ghosts also haunt nearby Gilpin Inn.

GILPIN INN

The Hotel has been the site of more misery than just gamblers losing their cash. A century ago, Lucille Malone was distraught over the death of her lover, who met his fate after being run over by a wagon. So much was her grief, she flung herself out one of the hotel's windows. And now it's reported that she still walks the halls.

Many reports, including those of the manger of the inn, say they have seen a lady dressed in black walk into rooms and disappear. Construction workers have met the lady in black while working on the hotel, and she has even managed to chase customers away.

PRIVATE HOMES

Black Hawk also offers many private homes which are said to be haunted. Cabinet doors have been said to open on their own. Specters can be seen walking through parlors. The town is rich in folks who simply say they have seen or heard something for which there is no earthly explanation.

A CASINO HAUNTING

Black Hawk also has an eerie report of a casino haunting. Guards have noticed on the security cameras a small girl holding a balloon. Nothing wrong with that except minors are not allowed to roam free in the hotel. Security workers were dispatched to the location and what they found was nothing short of bizarre.

With a guard at the controls of the camera they could see the girl, however in person, the other guards could *not* see her. Soon, the girl in the monitor disappeared, leaving only questions for the security people—with only one real answer, a ghost.

The bottom line, go to Black Hawk for a good time and remember you are always taking a gamble on running into a ghost in this casino town.

Next up, we head to a number of towns that contain silver, at least in their names.

Ghosts of the Silver Towns

After a few hours of listening to rain dance off the windshield, we exit a short ramp and find ourselves in the first of many silver towns in Colorado. All have some ghostly tale, none with a "silver" lining.

Silverton, Colorado, was once a bustling mining town in the late 1800s. The more than 9,000-foot-high city once enjoyed streets filled with activity from a growing population. Mining has for the most part left the city, but some of the early residents, they say, have not.

THE GRAND IMPERIAL HOTEL

The Grand Imperial Hotel is said to be alive with a ghost of a former guest. The guest room is believed to be haunted by a Dr. Luigi, who once frequented the hotel. Perhaps the good doctor will "see you now" if you come and visit.

Prostitutes once lined the streets in the city's heyday. The lives of many of them were harsh, and the lives of folks in those days were often cut short due to disease and living conditions. It wouldn't be a stretch for many a soul to stick around this landmark hotel.

The building has survived many years ,some with adverse weather. The ghosts of the past hang in the wings of this grand establishment, curious of the modern tourist.

If you don't want to meet the former residents in spirit, you can always visit their graves.

HILLSIDE CEMETERY

The Hillside Cemetery is home to the bodies of those long gone who helped found the town. Tours of the headstones of families of this past era can be taken. Learn the stories behind families who may not be as dead as you think.

Silverthorne is another town that is fond of its gravesites.

HANGING JUDGE SILVERTHORNE

The town was named after "Hanging Judge Silverthorne" who liked, as you can assume, to hang people in the late 1800s. The town has an annual ball to help raise funds to pay for burials.

The Coroner's Ball each year is an effort to generate assistance for families in need of funds to bury their loved ones. Participants have, in years past, dressed as famous dead celebrities and other themes—all for a good cause. The good Judge would be glad if you attended, and *you* will be glad he is long gone.

But of all the "Silver" towns, Silver Plum probably has the most active ghosts.

WEATHERDROP BED AND BREAKFAST INN

The town of Silver Plum sprang up like most of the other towns in the mountains in the mining rush of the 1800s. Many homes were built in support of the operations and need for housing. One famous for being haunted is the Weatherdrop B & B Inn.

The Weatherdrop is reported to be haunted by the ghost of a nineteenth-century miner. Guests say he likes to rearrange their personal items. And he likes to creep around early in the morning. The innkeepers warn that the ghost is very active and they don't advise prolonged stays, but will certainly oblige.

A SILVER CLIFF CEMETERY

Silver Cliff has a cemetery that is very illuminating. The graveyard is host to "dancing" balls of light that are said to move about around the tombstones. Critics complained the lights were merely a reflection of the town. They were not.

To prove or disprove the lights as having an earthly origin, a test was organized; all the lights in the city were turned off to see if the lights would disappear. They did not; in fact, they were as bright as they were before and they played about the headstones as they had been. And today, you might be able to catch them in the act.

Paranormal Platteville

P latteville was originally a trading post called Fort Vasquez in the 1830s. It grew into a city after the railroad reached the area later in the century. Many of the homes in the city are well over 100 years old, like Mamer House, which is 125 years old and has a ghost named "Ace."

MAMER HOUSE

To Jane Mamer, the fact that the house is haunted is music to her ears. And I do mean that in a literal sense. Jane has heard the tinkling of piano keys coming from the upstairs. As she starts up to investigate, the music stops. There is no piano in the house, so the music's origin is a mystery.

The haunting is more than music, though. Ace the ghost, named after Ace Campbell, one time owner of the house, has appeared several times to different members of the family. Pictures have flown off the walls, a sugar bowl took flight on its own—all believed to be Ace.

Why would Ace be angry? Perhaps he doesn't know he is dead and considers the Mamers intruders? Maybe it is not Ace at all? Who ever it is, if you stop to visit the Mamers you might just see a shadow on the wall or hear some music—all courtesy of the afterlife.

After you have had your fill of haunted harmonies, you can head for a true ghost town where there is a grave situation going on.

Central City's Lady in Black

Driving into Central City is like a scene from *Back to the Future*. You almost feel as if time has been peeled back and you will be greeted by a rustic Westerner surprised by the visitor from the future. And the word is, some of Central City's past residents can still be seen walking about the town.

MASONIC CEMETERY

The Masonic Cemetery in Central City is the resting place of many departed who have visitors, some of the guests may be dead themselves. At least, that is what the locals firmly believe about the grave of James Cameron.

Mr. Cameron died young at twenty-eight from what they said was "heart paralysis." Many attended the funeral, including a beautiful young woman dressed in black. No one knew who she was at the time, but her mysterious re-appearance each year leads some to believe she is a phantom from beyond.

Each year, she returns about the same time. Dressed all in black, she walks slowly and places blue flowers on the grave of James Cameron. She may be the ghost of a young woman who committed suicide after James married another woman. Could she be a ghost who even in the afterlife mourns the love she never had while alive?

The Ghosts Aren't Fair In Fairplay

O ur next town has more than spooks sporting about the place. Fairplay is said to be haunted down to the bone.

THEM BONES, THEM BONES

Buckskin Cemetery is home to the body of J. Dawson Hidgepath, where he lies—at least part of him. While seeking a fortune prospecting on Mount Boss, Dawson met an unfortunate end. He fell down the steep mountain side and died one hot July day in 1865. His bones, broken and lifeless, were buried in Buckskin, but according to the towns history, they didn't stay there.

His bones were reported to have shown up a couple miles down the road in the town of Alma in the bed of a dance hall girl. The locals believed it was a prank and reburied the bones back at the cemetery. But the bones would not stay there long.

Time and time again the bones of Dawson were found in the bed of some fair lady, and as much as the locals tried to dispose of them, they would re-appear. They even tried dumping them in an outhouse to no avail, as the bones came right back, appearing in more young ladies' beds. The story goes that Dawson was looking for a wife and that is why they believe his bones ended up in the beds of only women.

There has not been any reports of bones lately, but if you are a fair maiden, a warning if you stay in Alma or Fairplay, you might have an unwanted set of bones beside you in the morning.

The Ghost of Georgetown

Georgetown was the top silver producer in the Rockies until Leadville took its thunder in 1878. However, thanks to Louis Du Puy's Hotel De Paris, the town did not meet the fate of many mining towns after the rush was over. The town is still today rich in appeal and frightening fables.

THE EDWARD BAINBRIDGE CURSE

John Mickle's Saloon, in 1867, was the scene of a nasty murder, the result of a Scotsman with an unbridled temper named Edward Bainbridge. Edward was quickly sentenced to death for his crime. Just before the rope choked the life from Bainbridge and his body swung lifeless in the cool mountain air, Edward made a promise. He said he would haunt the town for all eternity, a promise, thus far, well kept.

One year after he died, his ghost came back and haunted the jail he was last imprisoned in. The stories go he banged on cupboards, made hideous sounds, knocked over chairs and blew out candles and lanterns. In fact, his poltergeist activity was so pronounced and prolonged, folks came from around Colorado just to see the antics of this outrageous ghost. He finally stopped his torrent but returned years later. Twenty years later to be exact. His ghostly image appeared, noose still dangling from his neck.

He has made a repeat appearance every twenty years like clock work for over a century. Mark your calendar and visit Georgetown on the next anniversary; you can be sure that Edward will be attending as well.

FULL CIRCLE CAFÉ

The Full Circle Café in town has yet more ghostly tales, albeit they are rumored to be fake. The TV series *Sightings* reported on the joint that is said to have fifteen to twenty ghosts. Some locals, it is rumored, had staged the entire haunting. A fact that I am sure is behind many a haunted tale.

Ghostly Golden

On July 20, 1881, an unfortunate pedestrian wearing a derby met his fate on the tracks running through Golden, Colorado. The massive locomotive plowed into the man strolling along the tracks knocking him far into the brush. A search yielded no body and the incident was forgotten until sometime later when the man returned, dead, of course.

The reports say that at that same spot, passengers would see a ghost wearing a derby with rotting flesh hanging from his bones. In fact, he's even appeared on the train itself, walking the aisles and scaring guests and crew alike. He kept appearing until his ghostly flesh had rotted into dust; and some say today, you can even see him on the abandoned tracks now, only showing himself as a ghostly mist or vapor. His essence must surely be fading in this physical world.

If you want to catch a ride on this ghostly train story, you probably have little time before this poor soul has completely disappeared into thin air, just like he did in real life. In Golden, jump on to Highway 93 that crosses where the tracks once lay. That mist may not be an upcoming storm.

HATCHET LADY BRIDGE

Another story worthy of only a footnote about Golden is that of Hatchet Lady Bridge. The story goes that the decapitated body of Adolf Coors' son was found under the bridge near Highway 285. It seems that, if you drive over the bridge, your car will "sputter" and almost stall. The only thing that stalls in this story is the facts.

First of all, the rumor has a Coors who is a teen, and it describes him meeting his end at the blade of a crazed witch, if you attach the "Hatchet Lady" to the tale. Nothing is further from what happened.

Adolf Coors III was driving to work in February 1960, when he stopped to help a motorist who appeared to be broken down by a bridge. It was, in reality, a kidnapper who tried to apprehend Coors for a ransom. Coors was able to get free of the criminal, who we now

know as Colbert, but Adolf met his end when the would-be kidnapper pulled a gun and mowed him down.

His body was later found in a dump, not under a bridge, and his head probably was separated during the attempt to get rid of the evidence. Thus, you can see the real story was liquored up a bit for no reason I have been able to find. I doubt the bridge is really haunted and the only mystery is why the killer of Adolf Coors III was freed in 1978. That, my friend, is the scary part of this tale.

Now if you want a more "amusing" ghost tale in Golden, go to Heritage Square.

HERITAGE SQUARE

Heritage Square today is a small but quaint park with rides, live music, beer, and souvenirs. The park sits in the foothills a mile from an abandoned subdivision developers never finished. While the empty streets of the subdivision are an eerie sight, Heritage Square gets the press for being haunted.

Many years ago, before the park, there was a young man who had fallen in love with an Indian girl. Mixed relationships were taboo and kept the couple apart. In a act meant to separate the two, the girl was hauled off and the young man gave chase on horse. Tragically, he was killed in his desperation to reach her. But death, it is said, has not silenced him.

Today, some say they can hear the horses and the cries of the young man calling for his lover. He may never find her, but you might just find a good scare on your visit.

Colorado's Alien Encounters

A liens are categorized as "paranormal" because they are out of the range of normal things we can explain. UFO encounters are distinguished by first, second, and third kind, depending on whether the encounter is just a sighting, an alien is seen in the aircraft, or (most extreme) someone is being abducted by the foreign visitors. Then I would suppose for this next story, there should a forth kind, which could be best described as alien slice-and-dice encounters.

SNIPPY'S END

Alamosa may have a few ghost tales, but this story was so unusual, it begged for inclusion in Colorado's strange supernatural history. It is the tale of Snippy, a horse who met an unfortunate and bizarre end.

On September 9, 1967, Snippy's shocking remains were found. While it is not unusual to find a horse's dead carcass, finding one in this condition was. The flesh on the horse's head was peeled clean down to the bone. In addition, the organs of the animal were missing. Not your average victim of a predator. About the only thing big enough to kill a horse would be a bear, and the wounds would be more akin to a horror film, not the surgical work done on Snippy. There were other oddities about this gelding's death.

First, was the fact that no other foot prints were found around the body. Whatever killed Snippy was light on its feet, or not on its feet at all. And then there were the bushes. The brush around the area was flattened as if something heavy had laid on it. And what's more, odd holes dotted the ground around the area. Could it be that Snippy was snubbed by aliens? Good question.

Either E.T, hungry for horse, flayed the flesh from Snippy or someone was playing an elaborate prank. We will never know for sure. However, many other tales of odd wounds to animals have hailed from Colorado as well. Some believe aliens; some think the government is experimenting. Whatever the cause, it is truly one of Colorado's mysteries.

Is this a real UFO? Do aliens visit our planet?

So Just What Are UFOs?

Until one lands on the White House lawn, UFOs will probably always be a mystery. They may be nothing at all; they could be from other planets, the future, another dimension, or Billy Graham even suggested that UFOs could be angels. So before we ponder any of these explanations, what is the technical definition of UFO?

Everyone knows that U. F. O. stands for *Unidentified Flying Object*. This simply means to air traffic control, *we don't know what it is*. There is credence that a lot of these objects are explainable natural phenomena. That is, swamp gas, cloud formations, and then some UFOs are most certainly government testing of secret aircraft.

But there is that small percentage of sightings that we plainly can not explain, i.e., pilots flying close to objects that defy explanations regarding where they came from. So, if there are some "intelligent" beings floating in our atmosphere, where do they come from?

The first thought everyone has is, well, they are from outer space. If that is true, they are from really, really, really, distant outer space. The distance so great that no known means of travel could get any life form from one star to the next in any timely manner. But then again, we simply consider them as being far advanced and have figured all the math to make faster-than-light speed.

But do you really think if a life form figured out how to travel that distance, that when they arrived, they would hide from us? It is possible super intelligence breeds a reclusive nature, but there is another possibility.

Scientists are coming up with plausible and incredible new theories. The theories are critical because our present view of quantum machines and relativity has a few holes. The search is on to produce a "theory of everything" which includes some models which could explain UFOs.

One theory contains other dimensions and parallel universes. In these theories, there could be many Earths, or other dimensions. Could the creatures which live in one of these worlds have found a way to come visit us here? And if they are visiting, do they prefer the Rocky Mountains over other destinations? Perhaps.

Colorado has been called the second Roswell by many. It has many sightings and is the setting for many tall tales of alien visitation and even close encounters of the third kind—that is, abduction. At least, that is according to Steve Nance who claims they took an hour from his life.

THE CASE OF STEVE NANCE

October the sixth, 1977, was a day in which Steve and his wife would never forget. They were driving back from a long trip to Kansas. And believe me, I have done that trip; getting abducted by aliens would be the only thing worst than the drive itself. After the extended tour of the endless plains, the couple finally made it to the mountains and to the location of their terrifying experience.

Steve had made it to the summit of a mountain on route to Gunnison. His CB radio began to generate a wash of fuzz when he and his wife witnessed a brilliant white light ahead of them. The greenish UFO shocked the couple, who later realized they had (like many others have reported) several hours of time that they could not account for after seeing the UFO. They believe they could have been abducted.

What makes this case seem credible is that many others saw strange lights that evening as well. The Salida police confirmed that many locals that night, and the days leading up to the event, had seen something. The reports were all similar: greenish, glowing object in the sky. Even the *Denver Post* had picked up the story, it created such a stir. But what is really bizarre about this UFO sighting is the local folklore of an angel that has been known to manifest at night.

The Angel Of Shavano is an ancient Indian legend of a princess who pleaded with the gods because her people were suffering from a severe drought. The angel was thought to be her spirit returning each year to once again petition for water for her people. Some say the "The Angel Of Shavano" is just melting snow—depends on who you hear the story from. The one fact that is true is that if you are driving down Route 50 in Colorado you could see something strange, be it nature or supernatural.

The aforementioned stories beg the nature of what a potential alien species could be like. Benevolent and malevolent tendencies are attached to most stories of close encounters just like that of ghosts. Let's take a brief moment to explore the possibilities of aliens, even existing before we can ascribe a specific nature to them.

The Possibility

Science is, as in the case with all paranormal phenomena, demanding of evidence—hard, cold, tangible evidence that can be proven. And aside from whatever "may" be in some secret lab buried in Area 51 we just don't have a clue, other than photos, personal accounts, and crop circles. There is simply no firm proof. But science itself asserts its theories with grandiose mathematical formulas and telling us we should "believe" something about a nebula in a distant galaxy without even touching it. Thus, we can apply the same scientific method to this subject with the same degree of confidence as our scientist.

That confidence is based in pure numbers and probability. The Milky Way contains between two and three hundred billion stars (2-3 x 10[11]), and there are some one hundred billion galaxies (10[11]). Thus, if the average number of stars per galaxy is similar to our own home, then the rough estimate is a total of 2-3 x 10[22] stars in all. Of that number some 2 x 10[21] of these galaxies have a "zone" where conditions may exist conducive to a planet that could sustain life. Further some 1 x 10[21] of stars have orbiting systems. Of those exoplanets, some 10[20] could have conditions (temperatures, chemistry, sunlight, and so on) that may be favorable to sustain life. The bottom line is some 10[18] (1,000,000,000,000,000,000 or one quintillion) have the possibility of having conditions for life. But even if there *is* life out there, there is one big problem: distance.

The distance to any of these systems is so far that the closest one to us could be at least 100 light years away—that is, traveling at the speed of light, it would take us 100 years to get there. So let's assume there is intelligent life. If I traveled 100 years to get somewhere, I sure wouldn't hide when I got there. Unless of course they are completely alien to even our own inquisitive nature. Ah, but yes, they *are* "alien."

The numbers suggest that it is plausible life is out there. If it has made it here is just beyond our being able to know. All we can do is look at pictures and speculate and listen to people's stories.

I will share one story from my sister, that has made me a believer in "something."

A Personal Story

One night, when I was about nine, I remember being abruptly awakened to the sound of my sister, her husband, and her young kids spilling into the living room. It was early morning, still dark, and I assumed the worse, an accident or something. But the story that followed was like something from a Spielberg movie.

Brenda and her husband, Bob, who is now deceased, began telling a fantastic story that their body language affirmed as being true. On the way home, a bright light that looked like a ball of fire could be seen over their car. At first, it was a curious site—a falling star perhaps, they thought. But when they turned the corner and it followed them, they knew this was no natural object.

Bob pushed their little car at speeds of over ninety miles per hour down the dark rural roads where the object cast an eerie glow around them. Each turn of the car, the object kept pace and drew closer. Eventually, they made it to our house and whatever it was inexplicably left.

The way they told the story was convincing—this was no helicopter or meteor. Their shaky voices chronicled an event that was truly traumatic to them. I have seen a bright meteor driving home down mountain roads in Colorado and the event is always brief, in fact, if you blinked, you could miss it. This was something, or maybe even some*one*.

Was my sister's family chased by an alien? Or maybe Government secret aircraft? Or possibly even a ghost? We simply do not know. But one thing is for sure, Colorado is a hotbed of the unexplained and maybe a favorite landing site for E.T.

Grand Junction's Ghostly Encounters

ENGINE 107

Another town with a tale of trains is Grand Junction where some say the echo of a phantom train can still be heard. On a cool night, perch yourself atop a cliff and listen closely. You just might hear a train that has not been running since 1909, at least in this life.

Unlucky is the word they used for Engine 107. That was an understatement. The train hit a boulder on the tracks, then flung helpless passengers to their doom in a horrible accident. This was after it had already killed many workers when it had run off a trestle earlier. That was not the end of the carnage; the train ran into a snowplow claiming even more victims. Thankfully, they decided to put an end to this train of death.

After so many casualties from this one locomotive, officials came to the conclusion this train was truly unlucky and retired Engine 107. But that has not stopped the sound of the whistle and steam engine from roaring down the tracks. Many report that you can still hear old Engine 107, perhaps the restless souls of her victims are still trying to find their destination.

Maybe one of those passengers is the famous ghost of Horse Thief Canyon.

HORSE THIEF CANYON

The canyon is connected to the Colorado National Monument. In the nineteenth century, the remote location was used for hiding stolen horses (hence the name) until the law discovered the place. It was promptly shut down and the thieves arrested, most likely killed for their dastardly deeds. But a horse thief is not the ghost that is seen here.

The spook that haunts these hills is that of a woman in a white dress. No one knows why or who she could be. Could she be the lover

of a horse thief shot here still looking for her mate? If you venture out on a cold dark night in the canyon, beware, and if you rode a horse to get there, keep an eye on it.

THE ELKS CLUB

Back in town, The Elks Club is said to have a haunted atmosphere as well. Shadow people have been reported creeping about. And employees have said trash cans take flight unassisted. In addition, voices of the dead fill the halls, and doors open and close on their own. The Club is alive with activity, but perhaps by folks who are not.

POTTERS CEMETERY

Clarissa Vazquez of the CCPI (Chad and Clarissa Paranormal Investigations) ghost investigators caught some ghostly action in Grand Junction. As seen on the photo, orbs appear hanging about at the Potters Cemetery. It is a small graveyard with only one headstone; the rest are wooden crosses.

The investigators reported their camera's batteries kept going dead and the flashes wouldn't work properly. There was a feeling that something was in the nearby woods; they decided to leave what they called a peaceful cemetery.

It's not the moon! You can see a large, bright orb in the upper center of this photo. There is also a small group of orbs to the right of it that are not as noticeable.
Courtesy of Clarissa Vazquez

GRAND LAKE

Grand Lake has another Indian tale. A battle between the Ute and Cheyenne Indians resulted in a horrible accident leaving hundreds of women and children dead. Enough to fuel a ghostly legend.

In the battle, the Ute placed their women and children on rafts to protect them from harm. Sadly, a great storm arose and sunk

the rafts, sending them all to their deaths in a watery grave. To this day, some say a ghostly mist will rise and float across the water accompanied by screams from the distant tragedy.

Breckenridge, More Haunted Heights

Breckenridge is a favorite spot for winter tourists. And it appears not only those living enjoy this mountain town. This rustic western resort has a history of horror that lingers to this day.

PROSPECTOR RESTAURANT

The Prospector Restaurant is a great place to snag a good meal and maybe a ghost. A couple walking outside the building were shocked when a woman in white walked out of the establishment. What was shocking was that she walked through the wall. The couple was even more surprised to find the ghost had a name.

According to locals the ghost's name is Sylvia, who apparently has been haunting the place since 1860. The story goes that Sylvia's husband-to-be was killed in a mining accident. Heart broken, the woman still wanders the premises waiting for her lover to return. Rumor has it, though, the ghostly lady is not only friendly, but down right helpful.

I suppose waiting for someone for eternity can give a soul some free time. So Sylvia has found ways to pass the days with good gestures. Some visitors have reported their freshly-done laundry folded and neatly stacked by an unknown force. Sylvia is not only helpful, the local paper reported she even saved the lives of a family in a fire.

The apartment the family lived in was once a boarding house where Sylvia lived. The current family's dog, it is reported, would stare into thin air with its hair standing straight up on its back like it had seen a cat. No one knew if this was the ghost of the young woman, but one fortunate night it is suspected Sylvia did more than scare the family pet.

The fire alarm went off in the middle of the night, alerting the family of an impending disaster. The family was able to get to safety and call for help. After careful inspection, a curious item was found. The smoke detector had no batteries! Was Sylvia trying to be protective of the family or maybe her own haunting grounds?

When in Breckenridge, venture to the restaurant for yourself; the prospects of seeing a ghost, I hear, are pretty good.

BROWN HOTEL

The city has another creepy joint called The Brown Hotel. Built in the 1880s as a private residence, the location was purchased and converted to a hotel by Tom Brown, who additionally created a bathhouse that drew a lot of attention to the establishment. But bathing was not the only activity going on in those days, to be sure.

A Mrs. Whitney met her grisly end at the hands of an angry lover in an upstairs bedroom. It appears the affair was staged to lure the lover into an evil plan. When the man found out, he was enraged and quickly took Mrs. Whitney's life. Her tormented soul is said to roam the rooms of the hotel.

Cold spots, doors that slam shut on their own—all attributed to the ghost of Mrs. Whitney, her plans never fulfilled, her soul cursed to wander the halls until judgment day. At least, that is what they say.

Boulder's Haunted High and Other Spooks

When you think of Boulder, at least for a lot of baby boomers, you may remember *Mork and Mindy*, the television show with a quiet small-town setting nestled by mountains that seem to touch the limits of the atmosphere. But Boulder has a much darker side that sinks below the polished look of network TV, one of ghostly encounters. One of those otherworldly greetings took place at the local high school.

BOULDER HIGH SCHOOL

Boulder High School has a theatre that they say can put on a show from the living and the dead. One night, after a late night rehearsal, witnesses say disembodied foot steps walked across the stage and the catwalk above.

The stage is not the only place spirits hang in the school. A tunnel connecting the dressing room and the theatre is said to make one feel a deep sense of dread and impending doom (kind of like the feeling when you get your cell phone bill). It is reported, but not confirmed, that the tunnels catacomb under the streets of Boulder connecting to the University. Could something diabolical have taken place in those tunnels? Or maybe Cockerell Hall near by?

COCKERELL HALL

The hall was named after "Theo" Cockerell, an internationally known entomologist, science writer, and a respected professor at the University of Colorado, Boulder. But there is no connection to Mr. Cockerell and the haunting that anyone knows about.

Cockerell is a typical university building, unless you run into a certain lady on the third floor late at night. People have seen a lady in white (why women ghosts wear white I will never know!) on the third floor, in the attic, or even the bathroom. There is no explanation as to why she is there or who she could be.

But don't think you can hide from Boulder's ghost by staying at one of the local inns.

BOULDER COLLEGE INN

Boulder College Inn, although a newer building, has a host of haunted happenings in its halls. Some are typical, like things being moved about on their own or odd sounds echoing in the halls. Elevator doors that open and close on their own are all too typical of a "general" haunting. But the Inn has a few uncharacteristic events that place it in an entirely new level of a simple haunting.

Smoke-like apparitions have been seen in the building, something akin to what you see in pictures of graveyard ghosts. Also, a strange red substance has been known to appear on surfaces, and there are voices when no one is around. But most disturbing was an event that made skeptics *see the light,* so to speak.

One night, every single lamp on an entire floor fell over inexplicably. It was reported to have taken two days to put them all back up. Like Boulder High, no one ghost is known to be the root of the activity.

Another place with a long-standing haunted history is the Boulderado Hotel.

BOULDERADO HOTEL

A worker, while making the bed in one of the rooms, was startled by the TV coming on by itself. The worker noted that, at the time, the hotel did not have remote control televisions—this was the early 1980s. Other devices fall prey to the ghost of this hotel, too.

That same worker reported that in room 304, the hands on an old grandfather clock began spinning like mad, making convulsive mechanical noises to add to the oddity. The worker fled at once in fear.

Another incident was not limited to inanimate objects. A worker in room 306 said she was awoken in the middle of the night only to find herself pinned by an unseen force to the bed. While the girl lived to tell the tale, the mystery of what happened lives in her mind. In fact, mystery envelops the hotel down to its wood.

It appears that the cherry wood that makes up part of the hotel is a complete mystery to historians. Where it came from, how it got there... The hotel was built in the early 1900s, but the dark cherry wood is a lingering mystery, not unlike why certain things take place in this hotel.

Guests have complained of scratching noises coming from the walls and ceiling while staying in rooms where people had committed suicide many years ago. No one knows if it is the ghost of the lost, forced to wander the halls for the act of self destruction. Even sightings of spirits are stranger than normal—if seeing a ghost could be called normal, that is.

The ghosts of a mother with a child have been seen around the hotel. It is odd enough to see more than one ghost at a time, but a mother and child?

The bottom line on this haunted hotel is that if you like your spooky places with a large serving of mystery, this one is for you.

But when it comes to scary places, nothing beats a mortuary.

HOWE MORTUARY

Howe Mortuary, in nearby Longmont, is spooky enough to make the TV series, *This Haunted America*. There are cold spots reported in the basement. Now when we say "cold" spots, yes about every house has a drafty area, but what is meant here is that there are places where no environmental explanation can be found for why it is cold. But the ghosts of Howe do not limit themselves to the basement.

Many sightings have occurred in the main lobby area. Even Mr. Howe, the founder, is said to haunt his own mortuary. Motion detectors and security alarms go off several times a month for no reason. At least no reason in the natural world, that is.

MACKY AUDITORIUM

The Macky Auditorium has plenty of reason to be haunted. In the early 1960s, a young woman was practicing late at night alone. The

Boulderado Hotel. *Courtesy of Beverly Silva*

janitor raped and killed her. Her blood still stains the floor where she died. And more than her blood is said to have stayed behind.

Sometimes, at night, you can hear opera music coming from within the vacant building. Could the young woman still be practicing, perhaps not even aware she is dead?

And further, there are reports of the ghost of a man who haunts the towers. Was this man connected to the murder?

Bigfoot Tales from the High Country

Bigfoot crossing sign.

There have been so many Bigfoot reports in Colorado's Rocky Mountains that, as you can see from the picture, they posted a sign to be aware one might just cross the road ahead. While this post is humorous, some of the tales are not.

CAMPING WITH BIGFOOT

One couple who dared the danger of camping at an extreme altitude came back from their trip with a real chiller of a tale. They said for days they were followed by "something." All they could see was the shadow of a large figure, always keeping itself from being in plain sight. Until, that is, late one evening.

Sleeping was made difficult with the mountain winds tugging at the tent. One of the hikers heard something outside, something deliberate and not natural. He poked his head out only to lock eyes with a huge beast with glowing red eyes. Facing this creature, he could only do one thing, zip up the tent and pray it would go away. It did.

Reports have come in all varieties from around the Rockies. Loveland Pass has reports saying the creatures use a pond in the Lost Creek Wilderness for drinking water. They say the beasts roar at hikers, chase cars, leave foot prints as their trade mark. This wouldn't be so troubling, except the reports have come from wildlife experts and scientists.

CRIPPLE CREEK FEARS

Another sighting was enough to make one man cry. A six-foot-five, 220-pound utility worker was checking the ponds around Cripple Creek, when he ran into one of the creatures. Even at his stature, the sight of the beast was enough to make him weep.

The man went home beside himself, telling his family of the horrendous encounter. It was so shocking, he apparently had no humility to show his feelings, even in front of children. It was for certain this man encountered *some*thing, something so fearsome it shook him to the core.

INTERSTATE CREATURES

The creature does not limit itself to the high grounds either. Reports say it sometimes wanders around the interstate highway. A group of young men was traveling up I-25, about 100 miles south of Colorado Springs. It was early in the morning, still dark, and they were tired. The passenger next to the driver's seat caught a glimpse of something extremely odd just off the highway, an ape-like creature, pure white with a black face standing on two legs. The man thought he must be seeing things until the group stopped for a break.

A few miles down the road, they pulled off to take care of business. The two stood talking about how exhausted they were and the passenger indicated he was so tired he was seeing a white ape. The driver was shocked to hear that his friend had seen the same thing he had, but because it was so strange, neither wanted to admit it. They discussed going back to look for it, but decided that with a sick friend in the car needing to get home, they should move on. This was not the first time the ape had been seen.

Unsolved Mysteries later that year did a story about the Colorado front range on a "white ape-like creature" that had been seen along the Rockies. Could these men have seen the white ape of Colorado?

EAGLE RIVER

It is pretty widely known that the famous California Bigfoot tracks that started the whole phenomena were in fact a hoax—a friendly lumber jack with a lot of free time and imagination. The hoaxer spent years strapping on wooden feet and running around in mud and snow, fooling everyone. Until science came in and debunked many of the incidents reported.

Some foot prints, however, leave scientists scratching their heads.

Keith Foster investigated the Eagle River foot prints and found several things that made these prints stand out. First, tests confirmed the "individual" making the prints would have had to have been 900 pounds or more. And the oddity doesn't stop there.

The prints show evidence of a flexible foot making the indentation. That is, this was not wood. If it was a fake, it would be something elaborate with moving internal parts. In fact, the ground showed markings indicative of someone "getting their footing"—that is, trying to recover their balance. Several other key factors make this case seem more real.

The location is extremely remote. It is only accessible to a few people due to private property and adverse terrain. In fact, it took the sheriff two days to get there. So why would someone plant tracks where no one would see them?

Then there is the history of the area. As far back as 1881, people have reported seeing something in the area. So you have enough for a conviction—physical evidence, eye witness accounts, and circumstances that lend themselves to deduce this was probably not a hoax. The question is, what was it?

PITKIN COUNTY

Another sighting typical of a lot of reports happened in Pitkin County. A couple hikers were stunned to see a large furry creature standing on two legs off in the distance. Their dog didn't bark, to their surprise, as it was the kind of dog that barks at everything. It was apparently afraid—a feeling shared by the hikers.

The creature turned and stared at them. At first, they felt it could be a bear, until it walked off, still erect—something a bear can not sustain for long distances. The hikers declined to follow whatever it was out of fear.

G.C.B.R.O

G.C.B.R.O (Gulf Coast Bigfoot Research Organization) provided a notable report from Fair Play, Colorado. The photo shows foot prints of a large primate along what is called an "animal highway"—a trail frequented by animals. Apparently one of the animals had large feet and walked upright.

The witnesses to the footprints also said that, while in their cabin, strange noises, like a dog mixed with a rooster, were heard. The sound was accompanied by a strong skunk-like smell.

HERE TO STAY IN A BIG, BIG WAY

The Bigfoot stories are akin to the UFO phenomena, that is, little tangible evidence is available, however, applying the same criteria we use in our courts, there is enough evidence to substantiate that, at the least, something unexplainable is happening.

There are reports from the world over threaded in history, in almost every culture, of a large ape-like creature. Some call him the

More footprints from unknown creature. http://www.gcbro.com/COpark001.html.
Courtesy Gulf Coast Bigfoot Research Organization

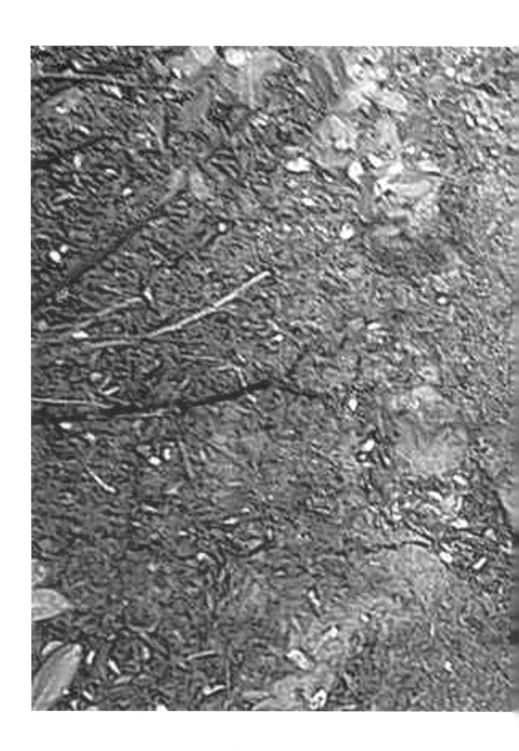

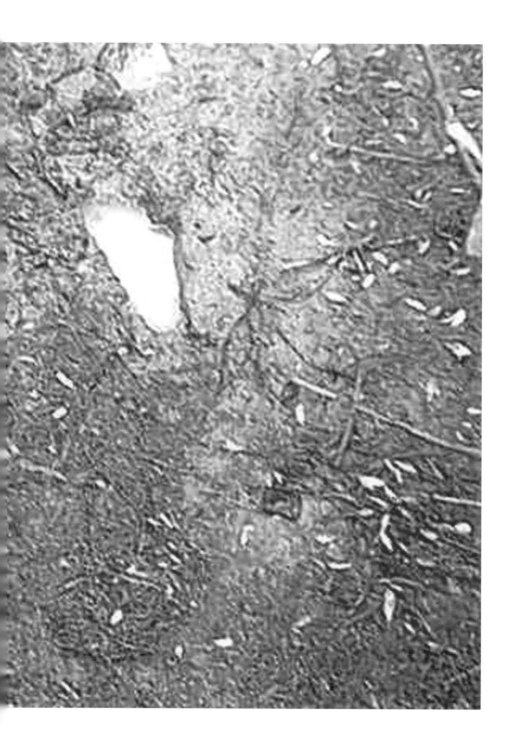

Yeti, some the Skunk Ape. American Native legends refer to Bigfoot as "Tak-he," or "Sasquatch," which means "hairy giant." The first white man to report seeing a Bigfoot was on Canadian soil.

In Alberta, 1811, Bigfoot was first reported to be seen by a white man. The event spawned not only the modern phenomena of Bigfoot, but the first hoaxes. The next big event in Bigfoot history was 1924, when a Bigfoot attack was reported. After that, the craze cooled until the 1950s when the aforementioned California hoaxer got things heated up again. But the biggest single event to spark the debate was the Patterson tape—one of the very rare sightings caught on film.

The problem stems from the fact that we still do not have physical evidence that such a creature exists. If, in fact, there is a species of creatures out there, they are extremely elusive. And if indeed they use the vast forests to hide, certainly they use Colorado's great wilderness as a home.

Creepy Canon City

CANYON CITY PRISONS

Canon City is famous for its prisons and the inmates in them—both living and dead. It is not a wonder ghosts would hang about in the halls of Canyon City Prisons. The prison has executed over seventy-eight people over the years. And the Canyon City Prison Museum is host to some of the manifestations.

Cell 19 is said to hold the soul and smells of a female inmate who once stayed there. You can even hear her hacking cough from time to time. Some have taken photos in the cell that contain orbs. Could this be the poor lady inmate still bound to the cell walls?

WOODPECKER HILL CEMETERY

Woodpecker Hill Cemetery is where they buried many of the dead convicts. Some do not even have names on the grave markers—just cell numbers. Perhaps that is why people see shadow figures by day and orbs by night. Just maybe these convicts are not wanting to be forgotten.

SAINT CLOUD HOTEL

The Saint Cloud Hotel, although not boasting the long list of the dead like the prison, has its share of ghosts. One is that of a little girl who is playing with her hair and then disappears suddenly. Indeed, the ghosts of St. Cloud are playful it seems. Many reports of mischievous activity, some familiar, like items moved and hidden are reported. Other reports of TVs that flick on and off by themselves have been mentioned, but most startling are the chairs that stack themselves.

HAUNT #22

Freaky Fort Carson and Fort Collins

FORT CARSON HAUNTS

Building 1047 in Fort Carson seems to have a good reason to have a haunting. A young solider was reported to have gone mad and killed several enlisted men. People say that you can still here the cries and feel cold spots. But the scare doesn't stop there.

In room 313 you can sometimes feel your bed shake, but the most frightening part of this haunt is the ghost face that leaps out at you in the dark. If you get stationed in Fort Carson, ask for any room but 313.

The Fort has other haunted tales as well. I suppose having a structure built on an Indian ground called "trail of tears" doesn't help in keeping the spirits happy. But that is where the government has planted one of its structures.

Soldiers say they see faces peering in through the windows and hear strange noises at night. They have found toys in a network of tunnels under the building, as well as, writing on the walls. Oddly enough, the writing made no sense, and later investigation found no trace of the writing at all.

FORT COLLINS HAUNTS

Avery House

The Avery House in Fort Collins is said to be haunted as well. It is said to be that of an unhappy child. Folks get an oppressive feeling walking into certain rooms. If you sit in the front parlor, you will be anything but relaxed; indeed people say it gets down right depressing, which they attribute to a presence.

Bingham Hill Cemetery

Bingham Hill Cemetery is what the dilapidated wooden sign reads. The cemetery is in about the same condition as the sign. You can understand why though; this place was an original burial ground for the early settlers when they died. And die they did.

When kids get sick today, we give them medication; they get better—no big deal. Back in those days, families were large just because about half of the children would die from poor conditions. And this graveyard was the place the sick, poor, and young were buried, including former resident J. Thomas.

Folks that come to the cemetery at night (and why would anyone do that?), say they hear children cry and "cold" hands touching them.

Cold Hands of the Dead

I am not one to doubt a cold hand from the departed can touch you—I have had it happen to me. I was about eleven and my then best friend began to act strange. He was afraid to sleep in his own room alone. He begged me to spend the night at his house for fear something would get him. I, of course, thought he had maybe seen one too many horror flicks, but what followed made me a believer.

We spent much of the night eating stale chips and sucking down enough root beer to make anyone jittery. But we soon grew weary of watching reruns and decided to go to bed. I laid down and thought nothing of my friends fears as I began to drift off into a deep sleep that was abruptly disturbed by something I can hardly describe to this day.

Like the folks at the good cemetery in Fort Collins, I had a direct encounter with "something." I felt fingers against my skin, but they were cold and unearthly. Almost steely cold electrical-like fingers were sliding up my leg.

Needless to say, I, in deep concern for my best friend, got up and left him immediately. I point this out because, in this book, I share a lot of reports where people hear something or see something and it just doesn't get the point across until you have experienced it for yourself. I have, and perhaps if you hang out in Fort Collins, you will as well.

Centennial High School

Centennial High in Fort Collins is yet another school that people say is haunted. A young girl tragically died from a fall from a fire escape. After the incident, an apparition was said to be seen in the school, and the school janitor even quit after an encounter with the entity.

Goat Farms

And you won't find fresh milk on one of Fort Collins abandoned goat farms, but you *will* see a white glob of *something* floating around—maybe. Reports are few and vague, but people say they have seen something in mid air like a white blob. They also mention jingle-like sounds, perhaps from a goat ghost? Okay, this story does sound like it needs to be put out to pasture.

Hell Tree

While we are on the subject of vague and unverifiable, the Hell Tree story must be told. It is rumored that a farmer in the 1900s would hang workers from a certain tree on his farm. Apparently, people got tired of dying and they rebelled, turning on the farmer and hanging him from his own tree.

And now, on a moonlit night, you might just see the farmer's rotting corpse hanging from the Hell Tree. That is, if you can ever find anyone to tell you where the *Hell* the farm is. All we know is that the tree stands somewhere in Fort Collins. Best chance to find it is on a moonlit night...but don't look for it alone.

HAUNT #23

The Apparitions of Arvada

COLORADO STATE HOME AND TRAINING

SCHOOL FOR MENTAL DEFECTIVES

This next story some say took place in Wheat Ridge, but some research found Arvada was most likely the truth behind this creepy haunted location. It was called "COLORADO STATE HOME AND TRAINING SCHOOL FOR MENTAL DEFECTIVES" but was known as "Ridge Mental Institute"—so named for the street nearby. The history of this location is fractured at best, but here is what we do know.

It was built around 1909. The residents were permanent, in that they would spend the rest of their lives in the institute unless transferred to another location. In those days, mentally handicapped individuals did not have opportunity in the general public, and aside from working on the school's farm, had not much of a life. But according to some reports, Ridge held more than just the mentally ill.

Reports from workers after it was shut down said normal children who were simply not wanted were admitted to the institute and simply forgotten. Even though they were normal, the state kept everyone drugged, and being in an environment of a mostly mentally-defective population, the children would grow up displaying the same traits of those around them. If it was true is not clear, but stories abound about this location—natural and supernatural.

Prior to the Institute being torn down in recent years, many reported ghostly encounters in the buildings on the premises. Voices of children could be heard echoing in the halls, including the weeping of a girl that comes from one of the rooms.

As mentioned before, some believe a traumatic event can put a signature of the supernatural on a location, a shadow cast through time as a reminder of a horrible occurrence that doesn't want to be forgotten. It could be the residents of the Institute want to be remembered.

And the spirits do more than make noise. This location seems to be a repository of all types of manifestations. People have seen "black masses" appear that resonate with evil. The modern version of *Haunted House on Haunted Hill* oddly enough was an old mental institute and the ghosts appeared as black masses. If Ridge is where the producers based the story, I am not aware, but the similarities are striking.

Others reported more than sound effects at the former house of horrors. The boiler room was said to grow "cold," accompanied by a stench. Is this the smell of a long-forgotten victim of some horrid crime? Still other spooks were said to hide flashlights, move items around, and whisper in your ear.

If you venture to the location, beware. The buildings may be gone but the former residents could still be around. And maybe, follow you home. According to some, walking in Arvada can be a dangerous task.

Assaulted by a Ghost

A story floats about of an Arvada resident who was raped by a ghost. The only other sexual assault by a spirit I am aware of is the famous *Entity* case in California. The following is a recounting of what happened.

It was the mid 1980s; a family had moved into an Arvada home. The sister began playing with a Ouija™ board, and one night, had a friend over to try and contact the dead. The girls played with the board like many do and didn't take it seriously, until the friend who was alone at the board made "contact."

She was sitting alone when the pointer started moving on its own. At first startled, she soon began taunting the spirit, making demands it make itself known. Her final demand, it was said, was that if this was a real spirit, it should come rape her, a request that was reported to have been fulfilled.

On the walk home that night, the girl was said to have been raped, and according to the story, doctors found no clear evidence of DNA. In other words, this was not human. But of course this is just a story, a rumor; this never happened. Or did it?

A Postal Haunt

Arvada's post office has not only a haunted facility, but a haunted worker. The local post office is one of the last places you would think to be scary. But word is, you can send express mail and catch a glimpse of a ghostly postal worker all at the same time.

The spook was supposed to be that of a cleaning woman who worked there. Supposedly, you can catch her mailing a letter. What is she sending? And to whom? No one knows, but when in Arvada, stop by to grab a book of stamps and maybe a glimpse of a paranormal postal worker.

Arvada has another story of mysterious mail as well.

You have heard of the headless horseman? Meet Colorado's headless mail snoop. Folks around town say the ghost of a headless man rummages through mailboxes along the streets after midnight.

And speaking of loosing your head, Arvada has another ghost tale or perhaps a ghost with a tail.

A Tale or Two to Tell...

There is a report of a female ghost that is part human, part goat. But that's not the strange part. The ghostly goat gal likes to sit in your living room and watch TV. And if that is hard to swallow, Arvada has another headless ghost story to reflect upon, or not.

Vampires, they say, can not be seen in a mirror. But in Arvada, a story of a headless female ghost can only be seen in a reflection. A lot of the stories I have just mentioned did not seem to rate very high on the validity or plausibility scale for me, until I came to the headless reflection of a ghost.

I want to share another story from my childhood. My sister would sit at her vanity brushing her hair each night. The vanity had a large mirror displaying a good portion of the room and part of the hall way. One night, while brushing her hair, she saw a boy behind her. At first, she ignored it, thinking it was me or my brother. It was not. She finally turned to find nothing but an empty room.

This doesn't mean the Arvada headless ghost story is true, but I know from what happened to my sister, there does seem to be something about ghosts and mirrors.

And finally from Arvada, my own haunted experience, which still lingers as one of the strangest events in my life. My friends and I were driving one night in a part of town that was mostly fields and trees. We pulled up to a stop sign with an adjunct street light when we noticed a bizarre event. The street light was shaking back and forth. We jumped out of the car to investigate and realized there was no apparent wind. How this huge light pole was vibrating in such an extreme manner was a mystery. We became frightened and sped off, and until this writing, have not spoken of the event.

And just as I did at that stop sign, we now leave Arvada. But the next city is no less haunted. We travel now a short distance to Wicked Wheat Ridge.

Wicked Wheat Ridge

W heat Ridge's population is packed tightly into a ten-square-mile area. Stories of ghost are almost as numerous as its residents. Most seemed, to me, more like campfire tales, but I've included a few of the most interesting.

This town is believed to have the oldest standing structure in Colorado, a log cabin. The Baugh cabin, built by a pioneer in 1859, still sits on 44th and Robb Streets. But the cabin doesn't have a reputation for being haunted, like the Richards-Hart Estate which is a typical haunted location—that is, orbs on photos and such.

If you want a ghost story that is not your run of the mill, head to Wheat Ridge Middle School.

WHEAT RIDGE MIDDLE SCHOOL

The school has a strange tale of young ghosts in the locker rooms. The ghost of a young girl is said to hang out in the dark corners of these rooms. They say the ghostly youth likes to wait until someone is alone and then scare the daylights out of them. But if you are a male student at the school, don't think you are safe.

Like the girls, the boys lockers has a similar tale of taunting spirits. The ghost of a young boy is said to linger about the humid halls of the showers. The ghost of Wheat Ridge must have a good reason to hang about such a smelly place. Only limited stories provide an answer.

It is believed that, on the premises on which the school stands, a shooting took the lives of those that haunt the school now. And not just in the buildings, but on the surrounding grounds. They say that the spirits come out at night and seem to love the dark, like the ghosts of the locker rooms.

A MOBILE GHOST

While hunting ghosts in Wheat Ridge, you may not have to leave the comfort of your car. A tale of the ghost of a woman that appears

in your car will leave you squirming, but not as much as the worms coming out of her eyes.

Witnesses report the ghostly woman will manifest in the back seat of cars driving by. Why she has worms bulging from her eye sockets is not known. She has been seen in the rear view mirror by the driver of a car and by other cars passing by.

Other local ghosts seem to fancy the automobile as well. Some folks say the ghost of a coal miner chases cars along dark streets like a crazed dog. How someone knew that this was a coal miner is a mystery. And what the ghost wanted is not known either. But if you don't see the miner, don't worry, there is still hope of seeing a specter. Just look for benches along the roads.

The ghost of a woman with a blue face can sometimes be seen at night on the benches around the city. Why blue? Perhaps because blue is the color of skin when you die. Or perhaps this is just another tale with no basis in fact. Only way to find out is to jump in a car and drive around at night in Wheat Ridge.

A GRAVE SITUATION

A graveyard within the city limits is said to be home to some natives—Indians, that is. The ghost of an Indian brave can sometimes be seen wandering among the headstones. He is said to be in full battle dress. Perhaps he is looking for the soldier who killed him in some long-forgotten fight?

If Wheat Ridge doesn't give you the chills you seek, there is still hope. Take a short ride down I-25 to haunted Highlands Ranch.

HAUNT #25

Haunted Highlands Ranch

T he most terrifying part of Highlands Ranch is probably urban sprawl and not ghosts. But amid the vast expanse of new construction and track homes you can still find a few places with some history—a history of haunting.

DANIELS PARK

Daniels Park is home to an old nineteenth-century armory. It is also the home they say of a ghost named "Kether." Kether, it is said, held to heretical beliefs of a coven who worshiped the god, "Set." Set was the god of the desert and chaos in Egyptian mythology. And chaos is exactly what Kether would experience at the old armory.

Kether was said to have been disobedient to the coven and was subsequently sacrificed on the rocks near the armory. Her blood streamed down the stones, ending her life, but that was not perhaps the end of the story.

On hot summer days, you can venture to the park and feel the rocks where she died. While they should be warm because of the blazing Colorado sun, instead they are cold as the lifeless body of Kether who once stretched limp across the bloody stones. And if that is not eerie enough, the stones even feel damp to the touch, as if her blood was still there.

An apparition believed to be Kether has been seen in the area. She stands on the hill, possibly watching the beauty of a Colorado sunset, longing for the life that ended here. You can venture to the park and enjoy it with her. Or head to the local high school in search of more spooky experiences.

HIGHLANDS RANCH HIGH SCHOOL

At Highlands Ranch High School you learn not only math, but also lessons in the supernatural. The auditorium, it seems, is the prime classroom for instruction in ghostly activity. The booth has

a mischievous poltergeist that moves items and even makes them disappear. Locking the booth doesn't seem to help, either. The haunting doesn't end in the booth.

The catwalk is host to disembodied foots steps that send chills down your spine and make the hair on your neck stand up. Cold spots linger about, waiting like a spiders web for someone to walk into them.

But for a creepy tale that has more history, head over to the old Kistler home.

HIGHLANDS RANCH MANSION

Highlands Ranch Mansion was owned by Frank E. Kistler in 1926, and was known as the Diamond K Ranch. Frank divorced his wife, Florence, who then moved out of the mansion, taking all the children except one, Julia. Julia loved her father enough to secure a spot at the mansion, but she would not be an only child. Frank had two sons with his new wife, but the love Julia had for her father was not returned.

Julia's emotional abandonment by her father left her lonely and depressed. She spent much of her time weeping in her room. She did not die in the mansion, but after she left and long after the premises were vacant, visitors say they still hear her cry.

Not only do they hear her, but some say they can even see her. The ghost of a young girl in a pink dress has been seen in the west bedroom by the balcony. Others say they feel her presence.

And one guest said the ghosts are right on time.

On time as in the mansion's grandfather clock that seems to be haunted. The guest reported the clock chimed when, in fact, the clock had not been functional for years.

But one of my favorite stories is the rosiest of all.

I have been in this mansion and it is one of my favorite buildings in Colorado. The fireplace in the ballroom is grand indeed and is the site of a spooky tale from one of the tour guides. The guide said that with all the windows and doors shut, she felt a burst of fresh air filled with rose scent against her face—an act appropriate for the sorrowful Julia.

A GOOD CLEAN STORY

Another story I have heard from Highlands is not about ghosts at all, just a creepy tale. An old home built in the 1800s still hosts members from the descendents that built it. One is a current resident who was said to be bound to the house—a slave to cleaning and cooking for the men for decades. The story doesn't talk about her ghost haunting the place, but her "sadness" being a living presence hanging in the air. Is this Cinderella story true or just someone's imagination? Or even someone remembering Julia's story incorrectly?

But back to hunting ghosts; we move on to another school with a creepy curriculum.

NORTHRIDGE ELEMENTARY SCHOOL

The cafeteria at Northridge Elementary serves more than typical school lunches; the menu includes some scare-filled moments. People say that the playground equipment doesn't wait for children to become active.

The sound of kids sliding and playing on the monkey bars fills the air, all in the absence of the children themselves. And when the kids are present, more odd things are said to occur, like the cafeteria lights flicking on and off.

Northridge is not alone in its ghostly population, nearby Ranch View Middle School has stories of its own.

RANCH VIEW MIDDLE SCHOOL

Ranch View Middle School has ghosts with the giggles it appears. In the halls, the bathrooms, just about everywhere, laughing ghosts can be heard. But for all the laughing, some of the pranks the spooks play are not funny.

Hand dryers come on as do faucets by unseen forces. The elevator is said to be an interesting ride. The lights will flicker, then the elevator will stop, only to suddenly start again. The control panel is ghostly; even when closed, the settings change by themselves.

Another spooky school in Highlands Ranch is Thunder Ridge High School.

THUNDER RIDGE HIGH SCHOOL

Thunder Ridge, like the aforementioned schools in Highlands, has those mysterious voices and laughter. However, here, the ghost of teachers can be heard. And in one part of the school, some say they have felt something flying past their heads. Perhaps something thrown by one of those ghostly teachers no doubt.

OVERLAND HIGH

Overland High has a sad haunted tale about its theatre. A student took his younger sister to the catwalks high above the stage to watch a performance one night. Sadly, the girl fell to her death.

Today, if you turn off the lights in the theatre and listen, they say sometimes you can hear her little footsteps on the metal catwalk. Now we move to a town where property value is far scarier than any ghost in town, that is Aurora.

SMOKEY HILL'S 7-11

Smokey Hill in Aurora has a 7-11 like most towns in America. But this one is special because in addition to hot dogs and coffee, you might get a free haunting with your purchase.

Patrons have heard ghosts calling to them as they leave the store and items have flown off the shelves—and I don't mean things selling well. The workers have a more chilling tale to tell of this convenience store.

Store clerks say that in the back of the cooler, glowing red eyes at times have greeted them. And footsteps can be heard when the store is empty. Why would this location be haunted? The store was built on the grounds on an old Indian reservation. A fact that supports other ghostly tales of Smoky Hill.

AN INDIAN MASSACRE

Just east of Smoky Hill Road is a location with a lot of troubling history. The story goes that settlers killed Indians in a battle. And to make matters worse, they came back later and murdered the women and children, too. This tale is the basis for present hauntings said to happen in the area.

They say if you stand near the place where the massacre occurred and start making noises, you will hear Indian drums. The louder you get, the louder the drums. What's more, if you stick around, fog might roll in, and just maybe the ghost of an Indian warrior will appear.

While it is hard to know the facts behind what happened to the Indians, there are modern horrors that can possibly account for some of the things heard. Local teenagers were killed in the area in a car crash. I don't know what connection the teens' deaths have with hauntings, if any, though.

FITZSIMONS ARMY BASE

Another scary location in Aurora is the old Fitzsimons Army Base.

The base is now abandoned—at least by the living. There is a building on the campus where it is said that if you climb to the top floor and look out the window, you will see the war dead walking about.

Nearby Littleton has a host of it's own spook-filled stories.

Littleton, a Tale With a Bite!

ALFRED PACKER

L ittleton Cemetery is home to one of the most famous cannibals in United States history, Alfred Packer. Alfred Packer holds the honor of having the first cannibalism case to reach U.S. Courts. But before we talk about what he is doing now, let's venture into the past and find out the story behind this horrible man.

He was born in Allegheny County, Pennsylvania, in 1842, and like many in his day, ventured west. Alfred or Alferd, as is noted on his tomb, was twenty when he set out. No one knows why his name is spelled wrong, other than perhaps an illiterate grave engraver, or perhaps Alfred couldn't spell his own name. If, in fact, he couldn't spell, it would make sense, since he chose an occupation in the West he knew nothing about.

He claimed he could navigate prospectors to ore, a desired commodity of the day. And, in the winter of 1873, twenty men from Salt Lake City hired him for a prospecting trip to the San Juan Mountains, not realizing he knew little of the trade.

In January of 1874, the group stopped in the village of Chief Ouray where they were warned not to try to cross until spring. Most stayed in the village, but Alfred and five others continued ahead into the mountains.

The spring came and the rest of the expedition followed to look for Packer and the others. Not finding them, a search party was organized to find either the men or their fate.

Packer, however, turned up at the Los Pinos Indian Trading Agency looking for whiskey. He appeared fit and trim, hardly a man who had been trying to survive in the wilderness. When he was questioned as to the fate of the others, he told several tales.

He first said he suffered a leg injury and they left him behind. When circumstantial evidence proved otherwise, he said that one of the members became crazed and killed the others with an axe, and he had to shoot the man in self defense. His story proved true only that they were all dead, for the spring sun would shed light on his lies.

Thawing snows laid bare evidence found by an Indian guide. Strips of human flesh, like sliced bacon, made it all too apparent what happened, as unbelievable as it seemed. In August 1894, the camp of the dead men was found and Packer was jailed in Saguache, only to later escape.

He managed to make it to Wyoming and lived there for nine years before being discovered. He was again jailed and sentenced to forty years, but oddly enough, was released in 1902, after a *Denver Post* worker campaigned for his case. It worked, and after leaving prison, he worked as a security guard until he died in 1907. Packer is buried in the Littleton's Prince Avenue Cemetery.

Now, after hearing the horrible tale of this "man eater," you would think his ghost must linger around his grave. But it is not his ghost that is said to haunt the cemetery, rather a goat named "Angelica" who was used as a medium to contact Alfred.

Does the ghost of this animal really haunt the premises? Why did they use a goat to reach him in the first place? You can take a trip to the grave and find out for yourself. And, if you are hungry, *The Melting Pot* is just a short drive. They have wonderful fresh meat on the menu, something Mr. Packer could certainly appreciate.

THE MELTING POT

Speaking of the Melting Pot, it has it's own ghost story. When I was there, and I have gone there several times, I only experienced some of the best cheese and chocolate on the planet. But the staff will tell you the dark side of the restaurant.

The location was once the old library. I personally fancy the twisting stairways and dark cozy rooms that now are a romantic dining experience. But I can imagine the place being haunted. And the workers will tell you they do more than imagine—they experience it.

Apparitions walk the halls and sometimes get nasty by tossing items around. The local residents are said to be well aware of the ghost. Could they be former library patrons? Or perhaps even former victims of Mr. Packer? I recommend making reservations at the restaurant to find out for yourself.

If you come up empty-handed, you might have better luck in Longmont.

The Northern Ghost of Longmont

L ongmont sits just north of Boulder; it was founded in 1871 by a group of Chicagoans. It was originally called the "Chicago-Colorado Colony," but later, was named Longmont. Like Boulder, it too has a good deal of haunted tales.

VANCE BRAND CIVIC AUDITORIUM

Vance Brand Civic Auditorium has a specter they like to call "Edison." Apparently, this ghost likes to cause havoc with electrical systems. It is believed to be the ghost of a janitor who was killed when a balcony fell on him, a place where he is said to still be hanging out.

Students have reported seeing a strange black figure on the balcony. In addition, Edison plays with the lights, moves chairs about on their own, and produces many cold spots in the building. And, oh yeah, then there is his dog.

This is one of the few animal ghost stories I found. Vance it appears has a guard ghost dog. Workers reported being chased through the building by the poltergeist pup only for it to vanish without a trace.

If animal apparitions are not your thing, head over to the Hansen Building for traditional spooks.

Satan Calling?

While this book deals mainly with specific locations, this next story, while it happened in Colorado, is not a phenomena restricted to the state. I ran across an interesting story about prank calls. Prank calls are not scary—unless they come from hell.

666

Tina (we will call her) returned to the dorm weary from study and partying. She immediately went to bed. During the night, she heard odd noises, strange but not alarming enough to pry her from her bed. She finally fell deep asleep until she was awakened by the phone the next morning.

She heard the answering machine pick up, but like most of us, she listened, not wanting to waste effort to run to pick up a sales call or someone not worth spending the energy on to reach the phone. The message was not what she expected.

The voice on the other line said, "Why won't you see me? Are you there? I know you are there." She didn't recognize the voice. Disturbed, she got up and went to check the phone. What she found was shocking.

First the answering machine did not record the message when she clearly heard it pick up. She then went to check the caller ID which read, "666." Tina reported that it happened twice, and it could be easy to pass off as just a prank or Tina making the story up, but others have said the same thing has happened to them.

Another report unrelated to the above incident said someone called them, no one was on the other line, but the caller ID was 666. An investigation left the phone company baffled as to how this could have been. But these two victims are not alone.

A brief search turned up others who have been plagued with 666 calls. I even found an explanation that the type of voices on the other end are evil if they are deep, good if high pitched, and so on. But why would 666 be significant?

666 is the number of man in the *Bible*. And bottom line, without getting into deep theology, no one really knows specifically what it is. It has always, however, been associated with the Devil. And in the book of Revelations, Satan makes everyone take the mark of the beast on their forehead which is the number 666—a number the Devil seems to favor.

If Satan really digs 666, or not, we can't say. Movies, books, just about anything that mentions Satan, utilizes that number to conjure up visions of hell in our minds. Why 666 would be on someone's caller ID, if indeed it is an entity calling, is beyond me, but I do have my own haunted "phone" experience so I can attest that demons like to use the phone.

A DEMONIC CALL

I was young, perhaps sixteen or so. It was a bright Saturday morning, but I chose to lay in bed and get my teen sleep (that is, I was lazy). As I lay there, a phone rang in my room. I didn't have a phone in my room. Then oddly enough, someone answered the phone (yes, the one that wasn't there). The conversation left little doubt it was demonic.

A voice snickered and said, "Hello, this is Billy Graham." This was said in a mocking way, trying to mimic this great man of God. Another voice was heard; this one clearly was a demon. The two entities started to argue and fight and the entire room shook violently.

The "attack" stopped, and I lay there puzzled as much as I was frightened. This was the same house where toys liked to wind themselves up; an evil presence *did* live there. I mention this story just to show that spirits do like to play with our fancy technologies. And sometimes they are evil.

So if you get a call, check the ID first; if it says 666, I wouldn't answer it personally.

Deep Fears on Barr Lake

For over a century, Barr Lake, just a few miles north of Denver has been a popular place to rest and refresh cattle, and in more recent times, a recreation area. But some say this is much more than just a nice place to take a boat these days; they say it is a place where the ghosts are present and violent.

This story is not about the lake itself, but the surrounding area. It seems talk among the locals has generated concern that something supernatural is going on. Strange eerie feelings, missing objects—typical for things you would expect from a haunting. But this haunted tale has a little more "punch" to it.

A female resident was cleaning her house alone one day. She heard noises that she generally associated with a ghost, but ignored them—that is until her cat began to stare into the basement and hiss.

The cat kept on guard, showing aggression to its unseen opponent. The woman began cleaning a bathroom nearby. As she leaned over with a mop in hand, something, or someone, struck her hard in the back. She quickly turned and found no one there.

The woman left the house at once (not sure if she took the cat) sporting a large red mark from being hit. She said she believed it to be one of three ghosts that live in the area. Especially, she thinks it was the spirit of an old man who planted a shot on her back. I do not know how she came to this conclusion.

There are few stories of ghosts that physically harm people. No one knows why a spirit would do that. Many think it is not a ghost at all when physical abuse is involved, but rather a demon or evil spirit. I support that theory and, personally, I stay as far away from those cases as possible.

Haunted Hamilton

This next story is admittedly short, but then again, the town is admittedly small. Hamilton sprang up over a century ago by the Hamilton Mining and Tunnel Company. You can only reach the handful of buildings that comprise the town by foot these days. The mining operation closed in 1905, but the activity has not.

The ghost of a trapper clothed in full buckskin can be seen from time to time by visitors to this long-forgotten town. He is said to smell of old pipe tobacco. While he is reported to be friendly, don't expect to get a good look at him.

The elusive specter likes to hang around at the corner of your eye. Just when you notice him and turn to look, he is gone. If you wish to visit the old trapper, make sure you come in the summer, in an all-terrain vehicle. If you don't see him, don't worry; the scenery is worth the trip.

Terror of Thornton

BRITTNEY HILL RESTAURANT

Brittney Hill Restaurant in Thornton has a tale of love, betrayal, and suicide—and of course, ghosts. Years ago, the owner of the mansion had a wife who had become unfaithful. He caught her cheating; the humiliation was too much, and she took her own life by jumping to her death on the premises.

Even though she had done great harm to him emotionally, he still loved her, and suffered so much, he too took his own life by hanging himself—perhaps to be with her in the afterlife. And maybe they are, for some say they have seen them.

It is said that if you look into the windows after closing at night, you will see the ghost of a man and woman embracing in the main lobby area.

RIVERDALE

Thornton also is the home of a haunted plot of land and a legend. A long stretch of road called Riverdale has a good deal of history behind it. The area was first used by Native Americans for hundreds of years before encounters with Europeans, who quickly took over and misused the property.

It is said that the land farmed extensively from 1880 to the 1950s used migrant workers who were abused. Also, many pioneers traveling the Cherokee Trail met horrible fates along the road. All events are believed to contribute to spirits that are angry and forever unsatisfied, taking their eternal frustration out on modern travelers.

But the traveler need beware the "gates of hell." The *legend* of the gates of hell, that is. The story goes that in the early 1980s, a cult group committed possible animal and even human sacrifices. And now, if you stumble upon where they once practiced their acts, ghost dogs will chase you and then suddenly disappear.

I lived in Colorado during the 80s and, in fact, do remember news reports of animal mutilations from time to time. If this was associated with the gates of hell, I am not sure, but I know someone was mutilating animals at the time. This brings an interesting question, can animals be ghosts?

WOODGLEN PARK

Woodglen Park is another outdoor spooky place to be in Thornton, or maybe *not to be,* that is. A tale of taunting resulting in death, or perhaps murder, lingers about this park. A young man was said to have been locked in an outdoor restroom as a joke. What happened was no laughing matter.

The building caught on fire, or perhaps someone set it, and the young man died. Today, the park is no longer there; the only thing that remains is a menacing-looking tree. If you walk through the area now at night, they say you will see something in the tree and hear screams.

HAUNT #32

The Gorgeous Ghost

I have already shared some paranormal train tales, but this next one has a special place, as the ghost in this story is said to be easy on the eyes.

Unlike the tale mentioned about the ghost rider with worms bulging from her eyes, this next spook had at least one man looking for another visit. It is about a train conductor who, while navigating remote mountain passes, picked up a passenger of the supernatural kind.

The conductor held steady at the controls of the massive locomotive as it barreled through the vast expanse of wilderness of the Rocky Mountains. The last thing he expected to see was a person on the tracks ahead of him. And this was not just any person, but a beautiful woman.

The train was moving too fast to stop; all he could do was be amazed she was there in the first place, and brace to hit her. His gaze of fascination and fear was broken when, seconds before running into the woman, she disappeared. Things would change quickly, however.

Before he knew it, the woman was standing next to him. She looked like something from a fairytale and smelled of fresh roses. He was drawn to her like a moth to flame. But inches before they touched, she was gone again—this time not to re-appear.

The conductor kept the story to himself for some period of time, until he heard others had encountered the woman as well. The story was always the same; she had an uncanny beauty. Was she a woman? An Angel? One thing is for sure, the conductor will always be looking on that route and probably be wearing his best aftershave.

Frightening Florissant

Costello Street Coffee House was built in 1886 as a humble home that was supposed to be a sanctuary, but instead turned into a house of horror.

James Castello, the owner, died in the home. His wife, Catharine, was burned to death—the result of a freak accident when her dress caught fire. Sadly, but not unusual for those times, two of their children died in their youth as well. Whatever the causes, this was a family who suffered, and perhaps their earthly home still echoes their sorrows.

The home is now a coffee shop. But the Castellos might just still be there. People hear footsteps running upstairs when no one is around. Toys play on their own without the aid of human intervention, items move about unaided, and the place just can't keep warm, no matter how high the heat is.

If you are driving through Florissant, stop in for a cup of coffee or tea and, say hi to the Castellos for me.

Spooky Summit Springs

A woman's grave marks the site of a horrible scene from over a century ago on Summit Springs—a scene that, to this day, the terror of what happened still lingers in the air.

The woman had been kidnapped by Cheyenne Dog Soldiers. The Indians were a type of resistance fighter for Native Americans starting around 1830. The Dog Soldiers' role was to stop the expansion of the white man west. They were noted for their aggressive fighting style, a point well demonstrated at Summit Springs.

The Calvary caught up to the Dog Soldiers at the Summit and the leader, realizing the U.S. Army would defeat them, slit the throat of his own pony so the enemy would not have the pleasure. The woman was already dead. Today, if you reach this remote location, you might just get a whisper from the past.

They say you can hear hoof beats at night and an eerie mist roles across the field. What makes the mist all the more strange is it ends at the woman's grave.

Ghost Gold of Poncha Pass

P oncha Springs is host to a tale of ghosts and gold. The U.S. Civil War seems an unlikely place to have any dealings in Colorado. But an interesting war mystery revolves around this tale, "rich" enough for a Hollywood movie.

The Confederate Army had sent a small band of troops to steal a shipment of gold bound for Texas. Most historians will tell you the war was lost in a large part because of financing, thus I can see why the South would be eager to land some gold.

The Southern soldiers intercepted the shipment on Poncha Pass but were quickly discovered and on the run from a Union patrol from Fort Garland with gold in hand. The Union boys caught up and a shootout left most of the Southern men dead—all but two who disappeared into the wilderness with a small crate of gold.

The dead were buried in Poncha Springs Little Round Top Cemetery where they are to this day; the Union Army searched for the escapees for days and they were never found. But that doesn't mean people don't see them.

Reports of an old man with a torn gray coat has been seen along Highway 285. People stop, thinking the man needs help, only to find he is gone. The local Sheriff has answered many a call about the old man and even a Boy Scout Troop has seen him. So who is he?

Some accounts by motorist say the old man is saluting as they pass by, a sure sign this could be our missing solider. I don't talk to the dead, but if I did I would ask the old man where that gold is.

Alarming Alma

A lma has a couple of good ghostly tales to tell; one is just downright infectious. That is the story of a Mexican sheepherder who brought more than sheep to town; he brought smallpox.

A DANCEHALL HEROINE

Smallpox in those days was a significant disease bringing many to an early grave before modern treatment was available. The little town of Alma was introduced to the disease in a big way.

Nearly everyone in the town became ill with the dreaded sickness. But in all the suffering, a heroine emerged. A dancehall girl took it upon herself to help treat the sick, nursing them back to health—that is, until she too became ill.

By the time she was taken down by smallpox, some of those she helped were better and wanted to return the favor. But she fled inexplicably into the mountains, never to be seen again. Never *alive,* that is.

Years after she disappeared without a trace, a beautiful veiled woman could be seen walking among the grave stones. But before you could get close to her, she would disappear. Is this our saintly dancehall girl? Is she still looking after those in death who she helped while alive?

In another tale from Alma, the citizens were much less charitable.

SCHWARTZ HOTEL

The Schwartz Hotel was the scene of a tragic family dispute that left a father and son dead. It is said they pulled their guns on each other and neither survived. Their tormented souls are said to wander the place still and have even scared people to death.

A woman who encountered the devious duo is believed to have hung herself after the event. How someone could come to that speculation is beyond me. I guess, as in a lot of the tales, you would have to simply go there and find out for yourself. But if you do go, I would leave the rope behind.

Wicked Wedding Bell's of Ouray

The Beaumont Hotel in Ouray was built in 1886. Back then it was called the Weathervane. The hotel was created to lure investors to the area during the gold rush. People still enjoy the rooms for all occasions, especially romantic weekends, which brings us to a story of lovers that is anything but romantic.

Most folks get "physical" on their wedding night. But one couple, many years ago, at Beaumont took the meaning to a new level. The husband, for reasons unknown, brutally murdered his wife. In addition to having to return all the wedding gifts, I would have to guess it was a bad night for them. A night they relive every year on the anniversary of the murder.

Each year, it is said you can see the young woman stabbed twice in the chest and then in her leg, then dragged down the hall, and hung on a hook like a slab of meat. All this took place on the third floor, so be aware to stay away during the anniversary of the murder.

It will happen at 2:14 AM; you will see her walk down the hall looking for her husband and then the gruesome show begins.

HAUNT #38

Eerie Elizabeth

Elizabeth is one of the older towns in Colorado; it was originally called Weber Sawmill, until the railroad caused the area to grow. When the population reached 200, it was named Elizabeth after Elizabeth Ray, the sister-in-law of John Evans, who was the Governor at the time.

Unlike Castle Rock and some nearby cities, it never seemed to grow up. Although modernization is slowly creeping in, you can still see relics of the distant past, one that walks around and has the name "George."

Buffalo Boyd's has one of the best Buffalo burgers you will find. I have eaten there often, but only knew of the great food. I was aware the building was old, but I didn't find out about the haunting until I had moved away. But they say the ghost doesn't show himself at dinner time, anyway.

They call the specter George. George has been behind much mischief at Boyd's. He has thrown pots, moved objects in plain sight, slammed doors and windows—the typical haunting signature. But this ghost did something a bit out of the normal in haunting circles.

A worker was in the basement working on copper pipes. The phone rang upstairs; the worker ran up to find a dead line. It happened three times. On the final time, when the worker returned to walk back down the stairs, he found the cooper pipes laying crisscross all the way down the stairs.

Killer Kiowa

Kiowa is a short drive from Elizabeth and more secluded. This remote location was once the scene of a slaughter of innocence. November 29, 1864, some 200 Native Americans were brutally massacred by U.S. troops lead by Colonel John Chivington. What is worse, they were mostly women and children.

The troops chased the Indians along the Sand Creek. The creek had small caves where they tried in vain to hide. They were pulled out, mutilated, used for target practice—even their limbs were chopped off and used as trophies. All acts hard to imagine civilized man doing, yet, it took place. And the memory, they say, lives on.

As if the Earth itself will not let anyone forget this inhuman act, each year, on the anniversary, they say you can see the women and children walk the creek. They appear only briefly and then dissolve into the sand. They seem not to want to frighten anyone, but merely to not be forgotten.

Floating Lady of Francisco

B uilt in 1862 by Colonel John M. Francisco and Judge Henry Daigre, Francisco Fort was a central location where the men could supervise a farming community in the Upper Cuchara Valley. The fort had one-foot-thick walls in order to protect against Indian attacks. While they were fearful of what was outside the fort at the time, these days, it was what was inside that made people run for their lives.

Two spirits are said to haunt these halls—the candle lady and the floating lady. In addition to orbs, cold spots, and mysterious flickering lights, you might just get a glimpse of the floating lady and candle lady. The problem with this story is I couldn't find "why" they call them that.

Did they get the ominous names from sightings of floating apparitions? A ghost lady holding a candle? The answers are simply hard to find. But the location is open from 11am to 5pm daily in La Veta, Colorado, at 123 West Francisco Street. Perhaps you can ask the ladies themselves?

Monsters of Meade and Mesa Verde

Meade is said to be the place of a horrible crime from over a century ago. A lynching was believed to have taken place near the local cemetery. Now, at night, if you stand still, you can see the mob and hear the cries of this unholy act. Another story, even older, comes from Mesa Verde.

The Anasazi Indians lived in Colorado between 200-1300 AD. They were hunter gatherers, descendents from the "Clovis" people. On their diet was mammoth, which indicates how far back their history goes. Don't think they weren't industrious for being ancient; these folks could build.

I visited some of the ruins from the Indians and found the architecture outstanding. I have no clue how they could have built structures that still stand to this day. In fact, some are so well built, you could live in them today. And maybe the Indians still do.

Not in the flesh, mind you. But folks say you can at times see one of the ancient people walking around the old stomping grounds. Ghosts from an ancient and mysterious past. Because, the fact is, no one knows what happened to them.

The entire population simply disappeared completely around 1600 AD. Oddly enough, they abandoned their homes, leaving behind all of their belongings. Many theories about the causes of their disappearance exist. But lack of evidence makes it impossible to know for sure.

Do make sure you stop by any number of the Indian cave and cliff dwellings in Colorado. Stand in one of the stone homes and be transported back in time. You will, for a moment, feel as if you are centuries in the past, and just maybe you will suddenly have a piece of the past standing next to you.

Guardian Ghost of Saint Elmo

St. Elmo is called one of Colorado's most well-preserved ghost towns. Several natural reasons exist for this, however, many believe that its ghost is what really keeps this town from fading into the landscape.

St. Elmo began as Forrest City in 1878. The haunted tale of the caretakers of St. Elmo began in 1881, when the Stark family moved to town. Mr. Stark (Anton) worked in the mines, while Anna, his wife, ran a general store and hotel called the Comfort Inn. The Starks had three children they raised in the town: Tony, Roy, and Annabelle. It is said they lived anything but a normal life.

Anna was said to be ruthless, without humor, and controlling. She didn't let her children associate with anyone outside the hotel. They lived in servitude to the needs of the Inn. Their Mother's fears of having the children influenced by outsiders would soon be in vain, as the towns people would all but disappear.

The mining operations died, and with no work, St. Elmo was almost deserted. The proverbial stake in the heart of the town was when the railroad was cut off in 1920. The town was isolated; everyone left but a hand full of people, including the Starks.

The Starks were said to have spent many years trying to bring development back to the town. They were successful to some extent in tourism, renting rooms to travelers until the death of Anton. After that event, things began to deteriorate further.

Annabel married and moved away, only to have the marriage mysteriously end two years later bringing her back. Her brother and mother both soon passed away, leaving Tony and Annabel alone in the midst of a ghost town—a loneliness that is believed to have driven them mad.

Reports say that the siblings lived in an unsavory lifestyle, both in their living quarters and personal hygiene. Annabel even earned the title of "Dirty Annie." She was still, however, liked and said to have been kind and caring nonetheless. The eccentric practices of the remaining Starks soon had them in and out of institutions and homes. Tony and Annabel both passed away, with Annabel being the last in 1960. But they say she didn't stay down long.

The Inn was willed to the Starks' friends, who moved in after Annabel's death. That is when the tales of the haunting began to surface. The first encounter was certainly a "chilling" one.

The new owners' grandchildren were playing in the room where Annabel had lived. Suddenly, all the doors slammed and the temperature dropped notably. The children ran in fear and refused to play in the building again.

Annabel and Anna were opposites in real life. Anna was an overbearing clean freak and Annabel, as mentioned, was a little more than messy. So this next haunting tale could have been either one of the lady ghosts playing with the new owners who were trying to clean the place up.

An effort to get the old Inn back in shape was hampered by some odd poltergeist activity. After cleaning during the day, they would put all the mops and buckets and such away, only to return in the morning finding everything piled in the middle of the room. Even locking the cleaning and repair gear up did no good; they would always end up laying back in the middle of the room. But the sure sign the place was haunted was in the 70s when a skier saw a ghost.

A woman was skiing by the Comfort Inn, which was vacant and locked at the time. As she passed by, she saw a beautiful woman standing at the second-floor window. The owners were out of town and no one else was around. The Skier said the woman was looking at a group on snowmobiles off in the distance. It was illegal for them to be there.

The skier went over and advised the group they had to leave. As they sped off, the skier looked back at the Inn and noticed the woman nodding in agreement. The woman then turned and faded into the shadows of the dark room of the hotel.

When the owners returned, the skier shared the story, and they all agreed this must have been the ghost of Annabel looking over the town. It made sense because, in her last days, she roamed about the town with a rifle looking for trespassers. Is she still protecting the area in death?

Thus, a word of caution. If you head to St. Elmo, Annabel will be watching what you are doing. So beware!

The Tools of the Trade

These days, ghost hunting is becoming a favorite pastime for many paranormal enthusiasts. And some have managed to make full-time careers on the subject. Many think that "ghost hunters" with camera and gear is something new, but the fact is, it has been around for some time in one form or another.

Of course divination and the occult have nurtured interest in the supernatural since recorded time. But the modern idea of using technology to bear evidence of the afterlife might have just started with Thomas Edison.

October 1920, the headline of *The American Magazine* read, "Edison working on how to communicate with the next world." Edison was a huge success at many of the technological advances that, of course, we all benefit from today. On this particular venture, however, he failed.

Many would wonder why such a great mind would be given to superstitious conjectures. Consider Albert Einstein who was probably the greatest scientist of those times. He had an interesting theory.

Einstein says that you can not destroy matter. It merely gets converted from one form to another. The human body is made up of organic and electrical energies. And, after death, these "energies" simply are rearranged. Edison used this approach for his ghost machine.

His theory was that these energies which make up a person— he called them "life units"—after death, are dispersed. His machine was an effort to detect these forces that had left the body and to communicate with them.

I can see from his perspective, with some of his inventions almost seeming *miraculous* in the day, why he thought he could do such a thing. And even though his machine did not work, a long list of other gadgets to help connect us to the other side have developed over the years.

Another name from the 1930s deserves credit for the modernization of ghost hunting; that is Harry Price. Harry also generated headlines, however, his were more dime-store-novel material. Early ghost hunting was birthed in the days of Houdini and freak shows, so naturally, there was a touch of the theatrical to it all. Today's ghostly hunters take a

much more serious tone in attitude and evidence, starting with the equipment itself. Let us look at a few of these items.

First, of course, would be a camera. Digital? 35mm? Which is better? I would think the higher the resolution, the better. Otherwise your images are pixilated. Some hunters take both a digital and a 35mm and compare later. Perhaps that spooky specter was just a smudge on the lens of the old 35. Having two sets of proof will take care of those arguments.

Then, of course, video. Digital video cameras are light years from what they were when *America's Funniest Videos* started popping out grainy images on TV. Today, video cameras have a great picture, nothing like the old VHS cameras. And most folks can even afford an HD (high definition) camera, as well. But a word of caution—for HD, consider you need an HD TV for playback, and if you are editing your footage, HD software with enough horse power to handle large amounts of data. If you are not clear on this, don't buy HD.

An important factor to consider in your camera is night vision—so in those late night ghost stake outs, you can film well into the night with little to no lights on. It may be more for the living than the dead; that is, shooting in the dark is not to disturb sleeping residents, as opposed to ghosts who probably don't care if the lights are on or off.

A lot of ghost hunters in fact take "lots" of video and still camera images. They might place a piece of camera equipment in a room all night in hopes of grabbing a ghost. The downside of letting a camera roll for hours on end is that you have to watch the footage later. Gets boring when you generally do not see anything, but if you like fishing, it is very similar.

Audio recorders are another staple piece of hardware for a ghost hunter. In order to catch those EVPs (electronic voice phenomena) you will need to capture some sound samples. Most seem to prefer tape as opposed to digital. There are several reasons, not the least of which is being able to remove the tape and labeling it.

The EMF or Electromagnetic Field Detector is vital for detecting the "unseen" forces the camera can not detect. It will detect fluctuations and help the ghost hunter locate energy sources.

Thermometers are used to detect those cold spots we have talked about. They come in digital and infrared non contact. The infrared seems to be the preference for most ghost hunters—mainly because you can scan a large area all at once and there is less time delay from getting a reading.

Motion sensors can detect movement in a room that should otherwise be free of activity—that is, from human intervention. You can buy sensors that have cameras built in so that when the sensor is tripped, you have a nice picture of the ghost or sometimes family cat.

Also on the list of recommended items are walkie-talkies, first aid kits, flashlights, and anemometers (is there a draft causing that temperature change?).

You can find many ghost hunting guides online and in book form. They all contain recommendations on collecting evidence and the best way to "catch" that ghost. But remember, this is not a pure science and there is not a definitive method. There are, perhaps, best practices that folks have discovered that you can follow.

The one thing that is vital you have is "permission" to be on the property—public or private. If you are not careful, snooping around without asking first, you could easily end up a ghost!

That being said, have fun and use your head.

Colorado Haunted Tour Wrap-Up

I f you think the tour ended abruptly, you are right. I have, in fact, only begun to scratch the surface with the many towns and tales that abound about Colorado's haunted history and present. And I am sure I will revisit and find more to share. Until then, I wanted to put a personal note on the stories I have passed on.

First I have to say that things outside of what I experienced myself, I can obviously not vouch for validity. And further, reading this, you can only take my word for what I have said. That leaves you in the driver's seat for what to believe. That comes with a word of caution.

As I mentioned earlier, for all the places mentioned, you will need permission to visit. Many of these are private property, and even public places have limitations for safety reasons regarding where you can go. Thus, use caution and be smart, not only physically, but in the spiritual world as well.

What I mean by that is, I believe spiritual matters are to be approached with care. Many of the stories I mention are fun, and the paranormal, in general, has a sense of wonder and excitement, but beware. You are dealing with a serious subject matter—one you need to be wise about.

Just like I advise on not trespassing on property of this world, I warn you not to cross certain spiritual boundaries. The living should never infringe on certain territories of the dead. What do I mean by that? Ah, you will have to wait for the next book to find out, so stay tuned.

Bibliography and Web Site Resources

Bigfoot Encounters. http://www.bigfootencounters.com/articles/
stein1.htm.

Bigfoot Field Researchers Organization. http://www.bfro.net/.

CCPI. http://www.candcparanormal.com/.

Colorado Places. http://colomar.com/ColoradoPlaces/angel_shavano.
html.

Gulf Coast Bigfoot Research Organization. http://www.gcbro.com/.

Haunted Colorado Ghost Towns. http://www.ghosttowns.com/states/
co/alma.html.

Haunted Colorado. http://www.hauntedcolorado.net/.

Haunted Places in Colorado. http://theshadowlands.net/.

Haunted Places. http://theshadowlands.net/places/colorado.htm.

Kane, Rebecca. *"Spooky Souls in Summit Spots." Summit Daily News*,
October, 2006.

Legends of America. http://www.legendsofamerica.com/CO-
HotelColorado.html.

Malevolent Alien Abduction Research. http://www.maar.us/steve_
nance_ufo_encounter.html.

PR LEAP. http://www.prleap.com/pr/41053/.

Pritchett, Laura. *"Resurrecting J. Thomas." High Country News*, March, 2006.

Rocky Mountain Paranormal. http://www.rockymountainparanormal. com/.

Science and Ghost Hunting. http://www.zerotime.com/ghosts/science. htm.

Spell Frye Ghost Web. http://www.spellfyre.com/html/places/placeslist. php.

The Haunted Ghost Town. http://www.prairieghosts.com/stelmo. html.